ESCAPE FROM PHONINESS

Escape from Phoniness

by
Aaron J. Ungersma

THE WESTMINSTER PRESS
Philadelphia

STANDARD BOOK No. 664–24857–8

LIBRARY OF CONGRESS CATALOG CARD No. 75–75651

Published by The Westminster Press ®
Philadelphia, Pennsylvania

PRINTED IN THE UNITED STATES OF AMERICA

To my esteemed friend

J. BENTON TULLEY

ACKNOWLEDGMENTS

As the publishing deadline approached, only the cheerful enthusiasm of the Secretarial Staff of San Francisco Theological Seminary enabled it to be met. My sincere thanks therefore to Thelma Furste, Gracie Jones, Ruby Egnew, and Maggie Arms.

I wish here to express my gratitude to my wife, Mary, whose encouragement to finish the manuscript of this book in the face of many demands on my time is the chief reason it was completed. I also appreciate deeply the editorial criticisms of John and Michael Ungersma, and the valued assistance of Professor David Halperin in preparing the manuscript for publication. A final word of thanks is due Prof. Benjamin A. Reist, who, busy with a manuscript of his own, daily cheered on the writing of this book.

A.J.U.

CONTENTS

1 INTRODUCTION:
   THE RIGHT TO BE—YOURSELF   11

2 THE HOLLOW SELF   29

3 THE PROBLEMATIC SELF   39

4 THE ISOLATED SELF   49

5 THE DIVIDED SELF   62

6 THE CONFLICTED SELF   75

7 THE RESPONSIBLE SELF   95

8 THE COMPLETE SELF   111

9 SUMMARY   124

1

INTRODUCTION:
THE RIGHT TO BE—YOURSELF

THE PURPOSE of this book is to offer ways for a person to escape phoniness in the face of many temptations today to play the phony. The goal is to enable him to feel more comfortable with himself by encouraging him to take an honest look within without being dismayed or discouraged. I am convinced that each human being is unique and that he has a right to be his own separate self. My intention is not to add one more volume to the long list of books on "self-understanding," though that term will be found and discussed here. The focus instead will be upon self-awareness and an appreciation of capacities and potentialities locked up within every self. Most of us are painfully aware of limitations and failures. Sometimes we attempt to hide these from other people. The bluff, the bully, and the phony demonstrate to the discerning person their awareness of inner inadequacy by devious and manipulative ways of relating to others. There are more satisfying kinds of communication than those of the bully and the phony, who in their actions serve to remind us that most of our feelings of inadequacy are related to early childhood experience.

Life asks that we grow out of the unavoidable dependence and inferiority of the child to the reasonable independence and superiority of the adult. Such an adult is, as one poet has put it, "like a tree planted by the streams of water, that yields its fruit in its season, and its leaf does not wither." Ways of encouraging growth are the concern of this book. A healthy tree needs, in addition to good soil, sun, and water, a pruning process. Pruning is not particularly distressing to a tree, but when applied to human experience it can be viewed as a painful thing to be avoided if at all possible. We prefer the familiar, dead branches of past experience, prejudice, and habit, and we fear the removal required for new growth. Some lives, stunted and misshapen by crises of the past, cannot endure the pruning and so may need a more heroic intervention in the form of psychotherapy.

Erupting from the twin volcanoes of psychiatry and psychology, there comes today a tremendous flow of information on the self, its development, identity, and maturity. Sociology and anthropology add their valuable findings and insights, and most of the discoveries of these behavioral sciences have been made in the twentieth century. This is not to say that all that has been learned is sparkling new truth. Much of it is but confirmatory of succinct, pithy observations of the "wisdom literature" of many ancient and diverse cultures, including the "mother wit" of today's black ghetto. The enervating and destructive powers of guilt and anxiety have been the preoccupation of scores of modern writers and artists. "The guilty flee when no one pursues" is an ancient observation of the effects of guilt. On the matter of anxiety, only recent decades have caught up with cogent writings on the subject produced by Kierkegaard a century ago. What is new on the present scene is that ancient truths on human nature have been confirmed as a result of rigorous research, statistically verified in countless laboratory and life situations. Sigmund Freud is a noted and influential pioneer in this work of verification.

It is important to remember that Freud originated not only his method of treatment called psychoanalysis but also a psychology that went far toward disclosing man to himself. Presently there is a growing disaffection and impatience with psychoanalysis, significantly on the part of many analysts trained in the Freudian tradition. But Freud's psychology and the light he has thrown on the devious ways of self-delusion are the foundation upon which most of the behavioral sciences have built. He is a mountain peak which the newcomer to the field must climb over, for there is no way to get around him. In Chapter 5, "The Divided Self," I have referred to Hawthorne's remarkable prescience or anticipation of some significant elements of psychoanalysis. The following passage is from Hawthorne's *The Scarlet Letter,* published in 1850, some seven years before Freud's birth.

"Thus Roger Chillingworth scrutinized his patient carefully, both as he saw him in his ordinary life, keeping an accustomed pathway in the range of thoughts familiar to him, and as he appeared when thrown amidst other moral scenery, the novelty of which might call out something new to the surface of his character. He deemed it essential, it would seem, to know the man before attempting to do him good. Wherever there is a heart and an intellect, the diseases of the physical frame are tinged with the peculiarities of these. In Arthur Dimmesdale, thought and imagination were so active, and sensibility so intense, that the bodily infirmity would be likely to have its groundwork there. So Roger Chillingworth—the man of skill, the kind and friendly physician—strove to go deep into his patient's bosom, delving among his principles, prying into his recollections, and probing everything with a cautious touch, like a treasure-seeker in a dark cavern. Few secrets can escape an investigator who has opportunity and license to undertake such a quest and skill to follow it up. A man burdened with a secret should especially avoid the intimacy of his physician. If the latter possess native sagacity, and a nameless something more—let us call it intuition; if he show no intrusive egotism, nor disagreeably prominent characteristics of his own; if he have the power, which must be born with him, to bring his mind into such affinity with his patient's that this last shall unawares have spoken what he imagines himself only to have thought; if such revelations be received without tumult, and acknowledged not so often by an uttered sympathy as by silence, an inarticulate breath, and here and there a word, to indicate that all is understood; if to these qualifications of a confidant be joined the advantages afforded by his recognized character as a physician —then, at some inevitable moment will the soul of the sufferer be dissolved, and flow forth in a dark, but transparent stream, bringing all its mysteries into the daylight."

A truism of Freudian psychology runs: "To know oneself is to be known by another." Hawthorne's Dr. Chillingworth was well aware of this principle, as the above quotation indicates. Freud felt that the best way to accomplish such twofold knowing was through psychoanalysis where the patient reclines on a couch out of sight of the doctor. The patient relaxes, utilizing free association of ideas and thoughts running through his mind, and is encouraged to say everything that occurs to him. The analyst remains objective, making interpretations at appropriate intervals. Vital also is the reporting of all dreams, and their symbolic meaning is explained by the doctor. This brief description does not do justice to all aspects of psychoanalysis, but enough is said here to indicate that the process is lengthy and expensive. In classic psychoanalysis the patient usually sees his analyst for an hour a day, five days a week over a period of years.

Many other types of individual counseling and psychotherapy do not require the client to recline on a couch. Therapist and client sit facing each other, and dialogue is the rule. Many practitioners of psychotherapy tend to ignore the unconscious memories and experiences of the past so stressed by Freud and they focus on present problems and future possibilities. Problems, attitudes, possibilities, and feelings about them are explored. Insights gained and the decisions made during the therapeutic interview are effective only as they are the expression of the client's own personal motivation to cope with life in more constructive ways. "A man convinced against his will is of the same opinion still," is an old saying that demonstrates the futility of authoritative counseling by one who "has all the answers." The modern methods of psychotherapy respect the client's opinions and attitudes, and changes from these are brought about only by mutual exploration of all potentialities by both client and therapist. Thus the resultant decisions are genuinely the client's own choices among alternatives.

In the face of the mounting demand for psychological counseling and psychiatric help, many specialists in the field of psychotherapy have turned to group therapy. This development is treated briefly in the next chapter with reference to its contribution to self-understanding. Like individual counseling and psychotherapy, group work has many theoretical backgrounds and diverse methods. The role of the therapist as group leader is more that of catalyst than interpreter or counselor. Leadership is shared with group members whose individual contributions, the sharing of experience, problems, and feelings, speed up the helping process. Even the most shy and inarticulate member of a group eventually is encouraged to speak up and divulge what is distressing to him and his relationships. Because several people can be seen at one time, the group method is economical in time and expense. Its success with problems of mental illness as well as with marital and other difficulties has led to its use in the educational world of the university and the high school, where its name usually is "sensitivity training," or "training groups."

It must not be assumed from the foregoing discussion that this is a book on psychotherapy, counseling, or "do it yourself" psychiatry. The purpose here is to aid the reader to escape phoniness by achieving a full awareness of his own self with its unique organization and capacity. My concern is to assist the person who is locked up within himself or, contrariwise, locked out of his real inner self, to achieve a real appreciation of his own human being, *to be* a person, to experience more joy in existing. Because psychiatry, psychotherapy, and related disciplines have done a great deal toward assisting in the task of self-discovery, they have been mentioned here as sources of many of the insights we have on human nature, being, and destiny. Hence these therapeutic disciplines are source materials for many of the ideas discussed in the chapters that follow.

"O wad some Power the giftie gie us To see oursels as ithers see us!" By capitalizing the word "Power," poet Robert Burns, who penned the above lines, implies that only superhuman sources can assist in self-understanding, but I have indicated several human sources that are available. Today words such as "supernatural" and "superhuman" are outmoded. Man, who circumnavigates the moon and collects vast knowledge about nature, still is impressed by the mysteries of nature, and an easy division into natural and supernatural no longer makes sense. Theologians who currently debate the "death of God" issue seem to make the same point: God is not isolated somewhere "above" the universe but is actively involved in nature.

Both scientifically and industrially man has probed the dark secrets of nature and has utilized every source of power he has been able to find. Men still living have witnessed the change in power from the burning of wood in steam locomotives to the harnessing of atomic energy to drive electric plants and ships. Apparently man is the dominant master. The almost infinite patience of the Curies, after much research, gave us radium. Decades later the brilliance of the mathematical minds of Einstein and others unlocked the secret of the atom. Cunning and often ruthless exploitation of nature gave man more power. But in sorry contrast to the vast power that man exerts over nature, and draws from nature, he himself has lost his own inner nature, his own identity—his sense of personal destiny. For millions, the inner nature—the self—remains unexplored territory, full of unknown dangers, hostile forces, fearful possibilities. Anxiety, guilt, dread, surge to the surface in modern man. He is unsure of himself and marked by a restlessness, uneasiness, and loneliness unequaled in all of his previous history. Instead of being shut up within ourselves, is it possible to be locked up outside ourselves—to be out of touch with our inner selves? A measure of a man's knowledge of himself can be seen in his way of handling loneliness. David Riesman has written cogently on the problem in *The Lonely Crowd*. Many who have fled the loneliness of the farm, the prairie, or the mountains have been dismayed to find a more consuming and bitter loneliness in the city. The crowd does not create companionship; rather, it accentuates the lack of anything resembling it. Even the most casual visitor to Times Square in New York City at any midnight can hardly fail to notice the frustration, hostility, and loneliness marking the faces of so many of the people who drift there. Yet Times Square is but a photographic enlargement of the inner anguish afflicting many persons in every city, and in the remote village as well. J. D. Salinger in his book *The Catcher in the Rye* not only has depicted the inner life of the adolescent but also has portrayed the devastating loneliness of life in the inner city.

Loneliness is many-faceted and arises from many sources, but its most prevailing and permanent factor is failure in communication with persons significant to the lonely one. Where a person is genuinely alone, as in the case of many in convalescent homes and county hospitals who have no living relatives, the situation approaches the tragic. But even here the person who transcends his personal fate by interesting himself in others around him can find meaning and surcease from loneliness. This is vividly shown in Michener's novel *The Fires of Early Spring*. The inmates of the county poor farm pooled their pennies and dimes to ensure the success of the first date of the young nephew of their grasping caretaker. The excitement and the joy that resulted from this simple enterprise and from their relationship to and communication with the young boy added sparkle and zest to the otherwise meaningless life of the inmates. In sharp contrast to such people who are genuinely alone in the world is the loneliness experienced by many people who have hosts of relatives and friends but are unable to communicate with them and honestly "be themselves." Familiar to marriage counselors everywhere is the problem: "We can't communicate." Marriage is the most intimate of human relationships, where it would be assumed that communication is automatic or built-in. But married people know that this is not so, and some of the loneliest people in the world are married to each other.

In actuality there is a great deal of communication in every marriage, but much of it is nonverbal rather than verbal. The slammed door, the silence, the face hidden behind the morning newspaper, the frown, the unnecessary absence, communicate far more eloquently than passionate prose or heated debate. I think of the couple who came in for marriage counseling at the marriage counsel center of the University of Pennsylvania. The husband preceded his wife into my office and took a chair facing a window. I seated his wife and sat down myself, noting that the husband's back was to his wife. He began the interview by saying, "Our problem is that we are not communicating." I turned to his wife, who agreed readily, "That's right, we can't communicate." After some silence I laughed and said, "It seems to me that there is a hell of a lot of communication going on here right now." The shock effect of this remark caused the husband to spin around in his chair and demand what I meant. I pointed out the eloquence of his treatment of his wife in his action of seating himself first and then turning his back on her before the interview started. This so impressed him that he turned his chair far enough so that he could face his wife as well as me, and the interview continued with more successful verbal communication. The loneliness of this married couple was caused more by their nonverbal communication than by what they expressed through spoken words. Once they had been enabled to express their feelings and attitudes honestly and openly in the presence of a third party, the marriage counselor, the seemingly insurmountable problems diminished to a size that could be worked on in a more harmonious relationship.

Matching the loneliness of the aged elderly patient and of persons unable to relate more adequately in marriage are the young who search for identity and meaning for their life. The hippie generation comes in for a great deal of discussion, judgment, and criticism. That youth are questioning the values and materialism of their elders is a painful truism which will be treated in a later chapter. It is important to note that perplexity of youth is not a new phenomenon. It is related to the necessity that compels youth to find a meaningful existence in relationship to the tensions of modern morality and changing values. The problem is an old one arising from deeper causes than just the changing modern scene.

Paul Martin Moller about a century ago described in his novel *The Adventures of a Danish Student* the difficulties of a philosophically inclined student: "My endless inquiries make it impossible for me to achieve anything. Furthermore, I get to think about my own thoughts of the situation in which I find myself.

I even think that I think of it, and divide myself into an infinite retrogressive sequence of 'I's' who consider each other. I do not know at which 'I' to stop as the actual, and in the moment I stop at one, there is again an 'I' which stops at it. I become confined and feel a dizziness as if I were looking down into a bottomless abyss, and my ponderings result finally in a terrible headache."

The practical man of affairs, energetically at work, finds himself quite impatient with the mental meandering of the Danish student. "Get to work, find a job, do something useful and your problems will go away," might be his advice. Yet Moller's student of the last century speaks for the youth of today, as Kierkegaard speaks for his elders. Shakespeare has told us that the world is a stage upon which each one of us is an actor. But what the student makes so clear is that we are not only actors but also observers of the drama being enacted. Man, who is certainly subject, can also make himself his own object— which is to say that he has a unique ability to get outside himself and take a good look at himself. The Danish student laments that he sees, not himself, but several selves or, as he calls them, "I's," and it is difficult to distinguish between them. A pathological extreme of this difficulty is discussed in Cleckley and Thigpen's case of Eve (*The Three Faces of Eve*), where the self seems to be organized around three distinct personalities. Years before Eve showed up in the psychiatrist's office the French doctor Morton Prince discussed the problem of multiple personality (also termed "dissociative reaction") in the celebrated case of Sally Beauchamp. Mental pathology, however, serves as a photographic "blowup" of processes operating in all normal persons, who do manage to find some sort of center of unity within themselves.

Could it be that the human self is multilingual, that it speaks many languages? It may speak one language to parents, another to friends, still another to the beloved, another to children, and a variant language to business associates. There is the "holy tone" that some religious people feel compelled to use in public prayer, as if God can be approached only by a special intonation.

When we adopt a different mask, facial expression, and manner to go with each language, it is no wonder that the self and its identity get lost in the process.

Language reveals many hidden aspects of the self. This is seen in the use of humor. One person's style in humor reveals a healthy personality who has realized joy in living. Another man's repertoire of jokes indicates a sad, lonely, bitter, and often sick self. Much humor is a safe way of making a sadistic attack on another person. The sexual side of human nature has its humorous elements and is provocative of endless anecdotes of widely varying qualities of humor. No apology is needed for earthy Falstaffian humor if we are to continue to acclaim Shakespeare as one of the great creators of English literature. But the man who knows and enjoys only the sick, sick jokes on sex reveals more of himself than he intends. The psychologist sees him as though he were carrying a placard inscribed: "Help me! I am miserable, lonely, loveless in my sex life." Humor, like language, is an extension of the inner self in its need and desire to communicate adequately with the other self.

I do not feel that the issue discussed here is one of many selves or "I's," or varying languages of the self. Even in the lament of the Danish student cited above, there is an objective "I" transcending, standing outside his dilemma, and passing judgment upon it. He was learning that one cannot become a true person in the isolation of his philosophical library, in isolation from other "I's." The self never comes into genuine existence apart from other selves. As Martin Buber has so exquisitely stated in his writings, the I is called into existence by the Thou. In the pathological case of Eve and of Sally Beauchamp the apparent "multiple personality" was resolved into one unified self through dialogue with another self, the therapist.

In this book the self is looked upon as a *unitas multiplex,* a unity in diversity. The civil war within, as H. G. Wells has described man, or the chaos of the id, as Freud describes seething forces within our unconscious nature, are one-sided versions or half-truths of man's inner life. Locked up within each self is a complex of capacities and potential gifts that also strive for expression and fulfillment. Lack of opportunity, education, and development of potentialities can cause very real unrest and dissatisfaction within and be projected onto the environment and one's fellowmen. Inertia, laziness, and lack of motivation also are causes of some of the vague anxiety and guilt that many people feel. They know somehow that they are gifted and have not made use of their gifts. Sometimes the tension caused by unexpressed creativity is released by explosive force, as in the case of the painter Gauguin. One would like to have recorded a conversation with him during his days as a bank clerk in Paris. In middle life he chucked it all—job, family, country—and went to Tahiti to paint. Though desertion of his family won him a great deal of disapprobation, he did win a new self and left a legacy of great art. Contrastingly the artistic sense locked up in Grandma Moses needed no volcanic eruption for its expression. In her seventies and eighties she almost single-handedly created the school of American primitive art.

This book will discuss the influence that isolation, divided-ness, and conflict have on the self, with the intention of con-tributing to the ongoing discussion of the problem of identity. The search for identity today has assumed extraordinary and sometimes alarming proportions. The sixth decade of this cen-tury is marked by vociferous demonstrations, the phenomena of the hippie and the dropout, rebellion and protests, and it may well be remembered as the decade of protest. It is reasonable to conclude that large numbers of the protestors, whether hippie or "The Graduate," are involved in a search for a more adequate identity and a feeling of personal worth and significance. Many of these do not seek professional help in their search. Their active involvement in the social and educational crises may be for them more helpful than conventional therapy. Other des-perately unhappy people, ranging in age from childhood years to what could be the serene seventies, seek help from specialists in human problems.

The familiar lament, "I don't know who I am," once thought to belong only to the crisis of adolescence, to be resolved by the adult stage, is heard not only from teen-agers but from adults of all ages. Erik Erikson in his *Identity Youth and Crisis* holds that the aging person either achieves a sense of integrity or, failing here, faces what life is left with disgust and despair. A sad commentary on this is the increasing number of suicide attempts on the part of lonely aged people. Education, status, "success," material security or lack of it, seem to have little bearing upon the high degree of suffering, unhappiness, and loneliness found in the life of those who have found no focus of identity or pattern of meaning in their existence.

There are those who feel strongly that the hippie and the dropout, in their quasi-Bohemian life-style, are thereby attempting to bypass the hollow values of the American way of life. However, many hippies in their lip service (and body service) to love, nature, and mind-expanding drugs demonstrate a pathetic unawareness of deeper responsibilities that love, nature, and the mind demand. That shallow values should be protested is good, but it should be remembered that the word "protest" originally meant to affirm something. On the mind: one sees little possibility of any affirmation of any kind of values coming from those who, in condemning the way of life of their parents, seek via drugs to escape from life and its insistent demands. On love: the psychiatrist Joseph Gutstadt remarks that the casual promiscuity of the youth he sees in his office is not so distressing as the utterly impersonal nature of their lovemaking. They use a word taken from the stud farm and speak of "servicing" each other. Anything even approaching genuine intimacy or personal relationships is lacking in their sexual activity. On nature: the hippie hand that offers me a flower in the Haight-Ashbury area of San Francisco goes with a face that is a mask of seething hostility. Lest I sound judgmental, which I do not intend, let me say that if ever a generation needed self-understanding and, still more important, a compassionate understanding, patience, and willingness to listen on the part of their elders, it is the hippie generation.

That a strong sense of personal identity is a most important value and goal is assumed in this book. In itself this value will

never guarantee happiness or abolish the inevitability of suffering. It can, however, enable one to deal constructively with the
unhappiness and the suffering that are inescapable in genuine
living and that the tensions of the twentieth century seem to
deal out in a generous measure. The multitudes lost in the
woods of identity diffusion can find a way out. Some will need
competent guides such as psychotherapists, unlike others who
will find their own way due to inner untapped resources of the
self, aided by the supporting concern of others and time for
maturation. Then they will be able to make the decisive choices
of vocation, avocation, values, friends, life partner, loyalties.
The adolescent approaches adulthood looking forward, but he
also is looking back to childhood, and the significant decisions
he must make for his life require all the help he can get.
I hope some of it will be found in the pages of this book, for
I feel a debt to modern youth in that they have made us keenly
aware of phoniness. "True identity depends on the support
which the young individual receives from the collective sense
of identity characterizing the social groups significant to him,
his class, his nation, his culture." I would add to the significant
groups those of his family, school, church, and community.

One of the definitions of the word "self" is "identity." It is
in this sense that "self" is used as a prefix in some hundreds of
words found in the unabridged dictionary. I feel that it is as
impossible and unnecessary to provide a comprehensive definition of self as it is to define love. Long before the existentialists
reversed Descartes's famous dictum: "I think, therefore I exist,"
the common man knew: "I exist, therefore I think." A most
basic assumption, though one often unexamined, is the fact of
one's personal existence as a self apart from nature and other
selves. Where this assumption is weak or lacking, there can
occur that separation from reality commonly seen in some
forms of mental illness. Where an individual is not fully weaned
from a parent, the self cannot achieve its fullest development
and expression of its uniqueness. This matter will be explored
in succeeding chapters that discuss the mass of theoretical and

practical knowledge on man that has accumulated in this century. But somehow this knowledge does not filter down into everyday personal living, interpersonal relations, and, where most needed today, international relations.

On the personal and interpersonal side, we know, or think we know, far more than grandfather did about sex, marriage, the family, child development, unconscious motivation, education, science. Our failure to integrate and digest this knowledge so that its vital juices can nourish us is seen in the variety of sad statistics on delinquency, divorce, drug addiction, alcoholism, and sociopathic anarchy. An agnostic friend of mine, professor in a great university, used to say: "It's fine to believe; it is better to know." Well, today we *know* a lot about what can make life more complete. Maybe it is time to *believe* that it can help us and time for us to go into action on the basis of that belief.

On the international front most nations piously proclaim a devotion to peace while devoting 60 percent of the national budget to preparation for war. Shortly before the onset of World War II, Professor Eric Jaensch, of Marburg University, said, "The basic difficulties between nations are not primarily political, economic, or social, but psychological." Psychology has taught us a great deal about origins of hostility and aggression in anxiety and frustration. But the chief use of psychology on the international front remains propaganda, brainwashing, and psychological warfare. Individual statesmen are well aware of the wealth of psychological information on human relations, but Machiavelli's practical primer for politicians, *The Prince,* after more than four hundred years seems to remain a standard textbook. Available in paperback, it is remarkably readable, and all successful politicians, it is said, are well acquainted with its directives for assuming and maintaining political power. In the turmoil of Middle East politics it is clear that territorial and political problems seem almost insurmountable. Beneath these lie the hate and fear engendered through many centuries of interaction between Arab and Jew. Psychology has something to say about hate and fear, but until these can be honestly faced and dealt with, little more than continual strife can be expected in this part of the world.

Men today are surfeited and weary with warnings concerning dire possibilities resulting from the breakdown in personal and international relations. The awesome consequences when emotionally disturbed men gain power over nations were demonstrated when Hitler assumed power in Germany. This sort of thing of course is not at all new to the historian. The Roman emperor Nero had some of the same personal problems as did Hitler. Nero demanded the worship of himself as a god and got at least lip service. Modern man knows that Hitler's megalomania was that of a disturbed mind, so there is at least some gain here. We may never be able to keep some paranoid politicians from gaining some power, but awareness of their paranoid ideas of greatness can guide us in our political action.

Much of what is going on in the modern world inclines many people to gloom and pessimism. Other people view the international ferment in a hopeful and optimistic way. Atomic research and bombs that created worldwide anxiety also resulted in radioactive isotopes for the treatment of disease and widespread industrial applications. An idea such as atomic fission in the mind of a scientist has influenced many lives ignorant of atomic physics. If anything is immortal, it is an idea transmitted from mind to mind. This is just as true about a useful idea as it is about a bad idea, such as the Nordic supremacy that Hitler tried so hard to prove.

There are a lot of ideas about the self, about man's inner core of being, that can help him as an individual and as a world citizen. All of them cannot adequately be treated in one book, but some important ones are discussed in this volume. In science an all-pervading idea is that of a unity or order in nature and in the universe. As Alexander Pope put it, "Order is Heaven's first law." We adjust our clocks by celestial observation and they are reasonably accurate. Corresponding to the idea of order in the universe, sometimes called the macrocosm, social scientists feel that there is a unity in the self, the microcosm. This means that every human being has his own inner, private, and invisible universe of which he is partially aware when he thinks, plans, or meditates. It also includes his emotions with their tenderness and violence, his hopes and desires, his prejudices, habits, sentiments, purposes, goals, and meanings. Though these often seem to be chaotic and to be working at cross-purposes, man still senses some kind of unity in all this which is his own self. Though H. G. Wells holds that "man is not so much a unity as a civil war," and Stevenson has dramatized the Dr. Jekyll and Mr. Hyde of human nature, we need to remind ourselves that civil war results from a breakdown in inner unity. The so-called split from reality seen in the mental illness of schizophrenia, or the multiple personality problem referred to earlier, also results from the deterioration of inner unity.

The marvelous unity of the human body results from an interaction of multiple systems. These are often referred to as the musculoskeletal system, the nervous system, cardiovascular system, etc. As an ancient writer observed: "I am fearfully and wonderfully made." One would like to surmise that there is a self-system, but there is no particular "place" to locate the self. The skeletal system obviously is located in the bony structure of the body. The problem of locating the self—if that really were necessary—is matched by man's attempts to account for the mind. Recent research on the brain shows that the mind is greater than the brain. In short, the human mind cannot adequately be accounted for solely in terms of brain states or activity within the brain. The gestalt idea holds here, that the whole is greater than the sum of its parts.

Decades ago surgeons discovered that the mind was not impaired by removal of fairly large sections of the brain. True, in some cases certain memories and skills may be lost, but in many cases these later may be regained and relearned more quickly than when first achieved. If one may not dogmatize about the mind, still less can one be doctrinaire about the self.

It would be nice if we could say that it is an emotional system, corresponding to the musculoskeletal system. But this would not be true, for the self is more than a collection of emotional states and possibilities, just as the mind is more than brain activity. The mind obviously needs brain activity to function, and the self is significantly demonstrated in the emotions and attitudes. Recent brain research also leads to one conclusion: the brain is "set" in some way, as far as learning ability is concerned, at about the age of twelve. Furthermore, this "set" is different for every single individual, so that no two people see or perceive the same thing in exactly the same way.

Uniqueness is another thing that sets off every human self from every other. No two people have the same heredity, with the single exception of identical twins, due to the "natural selection" of some heredity-bearing chromosomes and rejection of others at the time of fertilization of the ovum. If our brain development is unique—and our heredity makes us unique—our social development is a third factor in pointing up the existential difference of each self from every other self. Freud, and every developmental psychologist after him, emphasized that the earliest years of a person's life are of crucial importance in setting the pattern of life that he will follow. Erik Erikson teaches that one learns basic trust in or mistrust of his environment in the first years of his life. The environment includes people of course, and most pediatricians and child psychologists agree with Erikson. Facts of human existence drawn from a great deal of research and therapy with children support the theses of Freud and Erikson. These facts tend to make some theorists pessimistic about the possibility of effecting much change in human nature and behavior. Freud too was pessimistic but happily contradicted his theory in devoting a long life to helping and significantly changing people.

Let me conclude these introductory observations with the story of a young man of my acquaintance that is apropos to the concern of this book. A drug addict at sixteen years of age, with a prison record at twenty and an expensive heroin addiction at twenty-two, he financed his drug needs with a flourishing business in gambling and prostitution. Then he heard of the idea of Synanon, an organization devoted to helping drug addicts, and decided that a reorganization of his life, his self, was in order. Today at the age of twenty-nine he is an excellent and effective public speaker and a skillful therapist with drug addicts.

2

THE HOLLOW SELF

THE PHONY is the hollow man who can only "operate" among men rather than relate to them. It is not easy to detect him at first, for his hollowness has a smooth exterior, suave and seemingly sincere. Though he is often very intelligent, his intelligence usually is out of focus. He has more faces than Eve, is found in all professions, and infiltrates business and education. He is the despair of his wife, is despised by his children. Their love for him enables them to see through the smooth exterior to observe the hollowness and unrealized potential within. His form of communication is to broadcast two conflicting signals at the same time. Like the dog who growls while wagging his tail, you don't know which end to trust.

Psychologically the phony is an insecure individual who uses inadequate methods to achieve the acceptance of his colleagues and peers. (The psychologists ·call these methods "defense mechanisms.") Important among these is the manipulation of other people for personal or secondary gain. The phony remains hollow because he refuses to give and indeed often is incapable of giving anything of himself to others. Giving of self is necessary for sincere friendship and for all genuine interpersonal relationships. But some people in truth cannot give of themselves, for there is nothing to give. Therefore they resort to flattery, platitudes, and the accepted "in" clichés of convention in order to achieve acceptance. The phony knows how to "keep his cool" and he is aware, "man," that "grass" is not mowed by the "in" group but is smoked in some "cool chick's pad." The phoniest of phonies is the San Francisco version of the weekend hippie. Monday to Friday he is a respectable bank clerk. Friday evening he dons a false beard and "makes the scene" with the pathetic flower children of the Haight-Ashbury district. To meet the needs of this type of individual a flourishing business dispenses false beards, moustaches, and sideburns for the weekend adventure in make-believe life.

The authentic person is one whom you can trust. His genuineness is a firm basis of personality upon which enduring friendship can be built. Not surprisingly the phony often achieves success, status, and wealth but he remains a hollow man and is recognized as such by the discerning child as well as by the mature adult. The college dean in Ann Fairbairn's gripping novel *Five Smooth Stones* was recognized as a phony by students long before the administration was forced to take action.

Our culture seems to be one that puts a premium on phoniness, and the temptation to take this particular shortcut to achievement is all around us. The philosophers know there are no shortcuts to authenticity and to maturity, but we seek them anyway. Lincoln Steffens in his autobiography describes fellow students in the first psychological laboratory of the great Professor Wundt at the University of Leipzig. These men altered their statistical findings slightly in order to prove that their hypothesis was correct. This of course is a form of prostitution in science and it is not unknown today in education. A more amusing form of this activity is described by an archaeologist who found a religious fanatic busily chiseling away at the hieroglyphic writings in an Egyptian tomb. "What are you doing there?" demanded the archaeologist. The man replied: "I'm altering this inscription so that it will confirm my theories."

Most people are not phony, but an honest self-examination will detect traces of this form of character weakness in almost everyone. The conscious phony has one advantage: he knows he is playing his game according to his own rules. The rest of us often are unaware of phony elements in our daily existence. Being unconscious of them, we are vaguely ill at ease because of the unsatisfactory relationships that result. Occasionally we are aware of what is going on, and sometimes a sense of humor gives us objectivity. I shall never forget the surprise and then sudden feeling of warmth and appreciation that swept me when a brilliant scientist recently confessed candidly to me, "I guess in the classroom everyone of us must use a bit of bluff now and then." This man has a world reputation based solidly upon research and many publications. But he was not above admitting that he too knew the temptation to play phony.

A growing concern over this dilemma is also evident today. It is seen in the almost desperate search to escape phoniness on the part of many people. The extraordinary interest in group therapy, sensitivity groups, and "T-groups" is a clear indication of this determination to find a more satisfying way of life. Experimentation in a great variety of methods to achieve genuine relationships characterizes most of the programs at the famed Esalen Institute in California. Here in the rugged coastal region of the Big Sur area gather people who are sick of the hollowness, the sham, the lack of meaning in their lives. A significant number are members of the "helping professions": social workers, psychologists, ministers, psychiatrists. Some come away with the conviction and experience of a profound change in their life and attitudes. One professor in a graduate school left Esalen after a week there and declared that not only his whole outlook on life had changed but also his approach to teaching. Since he was a stimulating lecturer before his trip to the Big Sur, one can only surmise that his subsequent classes were livelier than ever.

There are others who report disillusionment with their Esalen activities. They state cynically that the good effects last only as far as the gates as one leaves the grounds to take up the difficult business of living in less exotic surroundings. Perhaps these people are the modern counterpart of those converts who were saved in the enthusiasm accompanying the sawdust trail evangelism of a bygone generation. I recall an alcoholic friend of my youth who could be counted upon to be the first of the sinners to come forward when the visiting evangelist made his appeal. Each winter, however, he backslid, to be converted again during the following summer when the evangelist returned with his tent and sawdust. The emotional zeal of the evangelist no doubt provided a shot of spiritual vitamins that lasted only until the harsh realities of winter appeared. Then only alcohol seemed to warm his heart and provide temporary respite from his problems. The concerned work of members of Alcoholics Anonymous finally accomplished for this man what a string of evangelistic tent experiences had failed to do. Perhaps the casual visitor to Esalen or to a similar center expects a weekend or a week of group activities to accomplish a miracle of personality organization. The shams and phoniness of one's lifetime cannot be erased overnight. The refocusing of goals, the integration of interests and capacities, the giving of the self honestly to relationships, require self-discipline and a lot of footwork that cannot be attained merely by jogging around the patio. After all, as modern, questing youth has it, neither a sunset nor a symphony lasts forever. The mountaintop experience may provide inspiration, but the cities, the factories, the people, the jobs, are in the valleys.

One special form of group involvement aimed at securing more honest attitudes and relationships is called the marathon. The process of group interaction in the marathon goes on without interruption for twenty-four hours, forty-eight hours, or even more. Intense feelings and aggressions are deliberately provoked as people have at each other with no holds barred. The success of the method seems to depend upon the skill of the leader or leaders, and also upon the motivation of the group members, their intelligence, ability to relate, and the amount of latent psychopathology that may be present.

Some very positive results of the marathon procedure have been reported. People have experienced lasting changes as a result of this effort to kill the phony that lurks in everyone. Others have found that it is all too easy for them to slip back into their old ways. In a magazine article in *Dare*, David French gives a very candid report of his experiences in a marathon, and in his appraisal he looks back nostalgically to those hours where he experienced himself and others as genuine persons. But as the marathon experience receded in time, he felt that his life continued very much the same as before his intense weekend.

Those of us who do counseling have an increasing number of clients who present this problem: "I have been to a marathon group," reports an attractive girl. "They took me all apart, and no one made any effort to put me together. Now suicide seems to be the best solution." The issue is put in various ways. A bright student who nevertheless was failing in all of his school courses tried a marathon. "They analyzed me," he declared. "Hell, I learned more about myself in forty-eight hours than I dreamed could be possible. But I'm all torn apart. Nobody there was interested in synthesis, in helping me suture the raw nerves they had exposed." The counselor then, himself an advocate of group work, and aware of its values, must proceed to patch up or to repair the clumsy surgery done in some marathons.

The marathon as a specialized "pressure cooker" type of therapy undoubtedly has some values for some people in that it enables them to take a long look at their real inner life. That it is equally valid for all people is a matter of doubt. If it is viewed as and deliberately manipulated as a new scientific gimmick, its leaders are open to the charge that they use (even with the intention of helping) people as things and objects instead of as potential persons and subjects. If as a gimmick the marathon holds out as a goal what I have styled "instant friendship," it is spurious. Genuine, long-lasting friendship with rare exceptions is not achieved overnight, nor over two nights. Hothouse plants may be beautiful specimens, but they usually are deficient in fragrance and wilt quickly when taken away from their protective environment. The marathon can be a shortcut to insight and can be valuable in clarifying attitudes, aggressions, and aversions, but it cannot provide a shortcut to maturity. Maturity, the mark of the genuine person, is not attained in twenty-four hours nor forty-eight hours nor even in a two-week intensive seminar or group involvement. It is a goal toward which one aims his whole involvement in the totality of his life.

The group process wherein the participants gather for a

weekly session of approximately two hours of intensive interpersonal relationships accomplishes a great deal in helping people focus their lives toward a meaningful existence. This is precisely because in the hours and days between group meetings "therapy" also occurs as one reconsiders, meditates upon, and makes personal decisions based on what has happened in the last meeting of the group. This is in accord with learning theory which is easily put on a graph. The new learning, whether a skill such as typing, represents a rise on the line of the graph (like a sudden rise in stock market quotations). Then there is the so-called "plateau"—the straight line where seemingly no learning occurs (where market prices remain unchanged). But it is in these "plateaus" where learning is consolidated, or internalized. The market investor, to push my illustration, must decide whether to buy more, to hold, or to sell where prices level off. Between group meetings one falls back to review progress made, mistakes made, or possibilities overlooked. The plateau is not merely a place for "marking time," but it is also a time for firming up what one has learned or has decided to become. This is a distinct advantage of ongoing group involvements—by whatever name—over the marathon approach wherein all must be settled, solved, and decided without the healing, meditative salve of time that comes between meetings of the group. Most counselors are aware of the fact that though the fifty-minute hour may be therapeutic, the 167 hours intervening before next week's appointment also present opportunities for changing, healing, and growing. In marriage counseling as well as in other types of psychotherapy it is not uncommon for "homework" on attitudes and activities to be assigned the client.

All that has been presented here is not meant to argue that only phonies seek out therapy, whether in group work or individual counseling. Indeed, the opposite is closer to the truth. Those who are aware of the shams so evident in daily existence, and who are determined to do something about the matter, are ahead of the rest of us who assume that phoniness is necessary or even normal, and therefore an inescapable part of life. Sidney

Jourard has written tellingly about the visit to the old home-town after decades of absence. Some old friends had matured and had become genuine persons. Others had remained filled with sham and were more self-satisfied than when he had known them in high school. Hobart Mowrer feels that neurotic and psychotic patients have developed their symptoms in significant part because of attempting to live by duplicity and role-playing instead of honestly being their real selves.

The great difficulties inherent in showing one's real self are evident to any intelligent person. Sidney Jourard has argued cogently that the way to selfhood and to health, physical and mental, is to be honest in self-disclosure to others. But very few persons dare take this path, and when they do, they quickly earn labels: "eccentric," "offbeat," "far out," and of course the more familiar "pervert" and "hippie." If any good is to come out of the twin phenomena of the hippie rebellion and the campus revolts, it must be seen in honest recognition of the phoniness in society and education to which these people are reacting. The fact that many overreact does not remove the real issue that they are raising. Throwing precious tea into Boston Harbor certainly was an overreaction, but it dramatized the rottenness in the politics of the day as it affected the lives of the American colonists. The violence of public and police reactions to the demonstrations of modern youth is proof of a thinly disguised fear that the sham and phoniness in our lives might be uncovered.

Because the remarkably able and intelligent youth of today are extremely perceptive, they can easily see through our well-built defenses, rationalizations, shoddy goals, and worship of the "bitch goddess success." Long ago psychologists determined that the peak of muscular and nervous reaction time was at about seventeen years of age. This theoretically should make the seventeen-year-old the best automobile driver because his reactions to emergencies should be the quickest. That statistics show a high percentage of accidents among drivers of this age simply demonstrates that other factors, such as caution, skill, and experience, go into the making of a good driver. In personal, social, and cultural matters our keenness of perception does not need caution, skill, and experience. Whereas skill may make the adult a better driver, perception which is based upon clear-eyed seeing and intelligence never will be greater than in the early years of life. If a person is found to be a genius with a high IQ at age twenty-two, he also was a genius at age twelve. I do not want to belabor the point that experience may make the youth more wise, but it won't necessarily increase his powers of perception. And it is in this use of the critical capacity of youth that the adult world sees great danger—the upsetting of old values and encrusted institutions. When personal phoniness is attacked or shown up it causes pain and it is normal to go to great lengths to avoid pain. To avoid the pain of self-examination parents and other adults counterattack youth with bitter criticism of their rebelliousness, or the parents subside into apathetic laments: "What did I do wrong?" "What is the world coming to?"

Picasso once declared vehemently, "All children paint like geniuses. What do we do to them that so quickly dulls this ability?" We might paraphrase this to state: All children are honest and keen in perceptive ability to see through the shams of much of our life. What do we do to them that eventually they learn that not honesty but duplicity is the best policy if they are to get ahead? The reported widespread use of marijuana, LSD, and other drugs in the colleges, the high schools, and even in the grade schools as well as among dropout hippies has produced many interpretations. Of these, two seem relevant here. Many of our youth use drugs, or defend the use of drugs as a symbol of their independence: "After all, Dad uses alcohol and cigarettes. Marijuana is not as injurious as alcohol, nor is it as addictive or harmful as tobacco." They obviously have something of a point there, as any honest adult is forced to admit. The use of marijuana and the more dangerous LSD, metham-phetamine, and other drugs as an escape from reality (if to the user reality means phoniness) merely complicates the problems of modern culture. One cannot combat or overcome the sham and phoniness of life by retreating into a fantasy world produced by drugs no matter how such world is rationalized as one that "expands the mind." One of the earliest apostles of the mind-expanding values of LSD—former Professor Timothy Leary—has yet to demonstrate the creative results of the mind expanded via chemical assistance such as LSD. Much could be, and no doubt will be, written about the prevalent use of various drugs in an effort to escape reality and its problems. But if the motivation for drug usage is that of one sickened by the phoniness so easily seen in much of modern life, this motivation should be recognized for what it is: a judgment upon the artificiality and hypocrisy of the life as it is in Western culture. A vast gulf apparently divides what *is* from what *could be* in terms of human interpersonal relationships. If this is what the Esalen people, the marathon experts, the counselors, the group therapists, the hippies, the drug experimenters, the college revolutionaries, are trying to tell us, maybe it is not yet too late to silence our angry, self-defense and listen. I teach in a graduate school the faculty of which was amazed, if not terrified, by a student demand for full participation in the educational process. This was some two years before the serious campus revolts such as those at Berkeley, California. The students demanded representation on all faculty committees, admission, curriculum, public events, etc. After lengthy discussion the faculty voted to permit student participation on a 50–50 basis. As a result, faculty members discovered in many cases that their committee work was halved by student participation, acceptance of responsibility, and suggestions from students. Phoniness masked by professional jargon is quickly exposed when students share a committee and when their votes carry the same weight as those of a faculty member.

Enough has been said here to point up the problem I have been discussing. How is one to face and to overcome the temptation to play the phony that is present in modern life? No matter how successful one may be in playing this or that role in life, the real needs of a self are not met, its full potentialities are not fulfilled, by role-playing. Apparently successful phonies are known as such by their children and they usually are empty and lonely people. Charles McCabe has said that "if you want some love, or some other little thing, from your fellows, you should play the game honorably. Give as good as you get." This is indeed sound advice, but like so much good advice, it is not easy to carry out.

A description of "the phony" has been attempted in this chapter, and a variety of efforts to escape phoniness have been sketched. These efforts vary widely, from the serious application of psychological insights by the professional practitioners at Esalen Institute to the desperate demonstrations and drug experimentation of collegiate and dropout youth. The way to the eradication of phoniness leads directly to the deepest areas of the self. The accomplishment of a genuine victory over sham and hollowness is possible. What Sidney Jourard has urged as a necessity in counseling as well as in psychological testing, the honest self-disclosure of therapist to client, is also a vital requirement in regaining a genuine appreciation of oneself as a person and not as a phony. The disclosure or unveiling of one's deeper, hidden self to one's own honest scrutiny is a painful process. It also is the only possible way to escape phoniness, and this will be discussed next.

3

THE PROBLEMATIC SELF

ANY VENTURE on the part of adults into that jungleland of modern psychology called self-understanding can, if it is successful, be considered a shortcut to maturity. For decades now, insights, findings, theories, and facts about human nature have been compiled by psychologists, sociologists, anthropologists, and philosophers. These last, along with the theologians, have been at the task of defining and explaining man for ages, but the newer disciplines have taken over and they have added a lot of spice to the compote.

Developmental psychology in particular has charted, literally in Erikson's works, and implicitly in the work of Freud, Jung, and others, the life of man from birth to the grave. These charts, when faithfully consulted and followed by the navigator, really do lead one to a reasonably secure and mature life as an adult. But skills in navigation vary tremendously, and knowledge of the charts of human existence does not always filter down to the real persons who could profit from it. Like a ship at sea that occasionally may be found to be miles off course the land dweller may misread or ignore the charts, lose his way, and find life utterly meaningless. He can then become a problem to himself and often enough to others.

The problem of being human sometimes is complicated by the very experts who seek to solve our problems. Parents, belatedly informed on the latest findings, usually via newspaper and magazine columns of psychological advice, often are overcome by anxiety as they contemplate the many mistakes they obviously have made in raising their children. This is because newspaper and periodical columns, though often of high caliber, are necessarily too brief to discuss thoroughly the implications of the problems. The net result is that parents themselves are traumatized as they contemplate the "traumas" they may have unknowingly inflicted upon their children. When parents and other adults consider their own chances for security and maturity, as they contemplate the findings of the experts, they may be swept with feelings of hopelessness or despair. They cannot live their lives over again and thus profit from the new wisdom concerning the developmental periods of life. To the demand, "You must be born anew," Nicodemus countered with the query "How can a man be born when he is old?" The answer to the question stated unequivocally that the second birth was a matter of spiritual living and relationship to God. The eminent Harvard psychologist and philosopher William James in his pioneer writings on the psychology of religious experience no doubt was aware of the Nicodemus incident when he described once-born and twice-born types. His differentiation centered on the degree of inner turmoil that accompanied the experience of the twice-born.

From the question of Nicodemus and suggestions coming from the research of James one might conclude that a second birth is simply a matter of making a fresh start. After all, the physiologists long have been telling us of the amazing capacity of the human body to renew itself. The processes of renewal are also possessed by the mental and emotional powers of man and these are utilized when he brings into play his so-called defense mechanisms. These are unconscious psychological devices that a person uses to ward off threats to what inner security and self-esteem he may possess. An unconscious process is, however, of little help to the man who wants rationally to learn from experience, and apply the new wisdom referred to above.

Taking a fresh start is not so easy, due to unconscious influences on a person's actions. One fact that stands in the way of his achieving insight and mature self-knowledge is the kind of stereotyped individualism that leaves man alone, *lacking in true individuality,* isolated, alienated from nature, from self, from fellowman, and from God. This is seen in the paradox revolving about the fact that this age knows an unparalleled advance in communications of all kinds, mechanical and personal, and simultaneously sees untold thousands struggling with the problem of identity which cannot be solved apart from genuine communication. Men who are not sure of their identity ("Who am I?" or "What am I?") are certain to run the gamut of life's difficulties without the resources that an adequate self-understanding could provide.

Definitely associated with the identity problem are the resurgence of glossolalia within the church and the extraordinary fascination outside the church with hallucinogenic drugs such as the mind-expanding LSD. Glossolalia, or speaking in tongues, has been in the church since the first century, but it is no unique Christian phenomenon. Ecstatic utterance has been around a long time and was part of the window dressing of many ancient religions. Though Huxley only recently discovered his magic mushrooms and Dr. Leary pounced upon LSD as the chemical shortcut to identity, the Great Plains Indians happily have been nibbling peyote for centuries, and the Aztec and the Maya, millennia ago, incorporated hallucinogenic plants in their religious cults. Psychiatrists for decades have been aware of the mind-altering powers of the modern drug derivatives, and have proceeded very cautiously with their use because of dangers which even the enthusiasts admit. The experience that results in glossolalia and the mystical indescribable effects of LSD may indeed enrich one's identity or even help one to find it. What is psychologically curious is the cult aspect of each of these experiences. It is my thesis that identity is not something that is "found," and this will be discussed later. But if identity, whatever it is for the moment, is to depend upon an esoteric religious cult or upon a chemical of the ingroup (who already have their own names for nonusers), it is likely to be an uncertain thing, or similar to Freud's "analysis interminable."

Another fact that seems to hinder adequate self-understanding is a sad acquiescence to the deterministic philosophy that underlies nineteenth-century science and that extends often enough unexamined into twentieth-century thinking. One of the ironies of this period of history is that the Calvinistic idea of predestination with its harsh implications was dismissed only to be replaced with a determinism far more implacable than anything Calvin ever dreamed up, and reinforced by all the prestige of scientific methodology. After all, Calvin's idea of predestination was somehow bound up with the providence of a personal God whose good will is stronger than evil, but scientific determinism is as inexorable and implacable as the ancient idea of fate. Indeed, Freud's psychology, which has been criticized more for its pandeterminism than for its pansexuality, draws on the Greek idea of fate exemplified in the myth of Oedipus for one of its central theses.

The Freudian psychology taught that a person's very earliest years are profoundly determinative for the rest of his life because, Freud believed, a person's basic character structure is fixed more or less permanently in the years of early childhood. This teaching is reminiscent of the old saying attributed to Catholic teachers: "Give us a child until he is eight and he will always remain Catholic." It is certainly true that familial influences and religious training, or their lack, are profoundly significant in the formulation of a person's basic character structure and attitudes. But it does not follow that he is thereby cast into a rigid mold, whether religious or psychological, from which there is to be no escape or deviation. It happens that adult Catholics have embraced Protestantism and in considerable numbers. Oliver Twist, despite the nimble-fingered companions of his youth, seems to have developed into a stable law-abiding citizen. Every community of any size knows adults who have achieved a genuine maturity in spite of often appalling backgrounds. Freud's basic pessimism concerning human nature was matched by a happy inconsistency, for he devoted a long life to psychoanalysis aimed at helping people to overcome effects of early traumatic experiences that had warped their lives.

The question at issue is not, "Can man change?" but more to the point, "How high is the motivation for change?" Every psychotherapist who has worked with alcoholics or homosexuals knows how vitally important is a desire to change, if anything permanent is to be accomplished. Today the deterministic background of much modern thinking increasingly is being questioned in many of the sciences, for we have learned that even atoms do not behave according to known scientific laws. If atoms seem capable of "free" activity, man certainly retains some capacity for free choice and responsible decision. This is a central emphasis of most of the modern existentialist writers. The adult, it is true, may be to a considerable extent determined by the early formulative years of childhood, but this fact does not present an insurmountable barrier to adult decision for change when motivation is strong for such change.

The old platitude, "You can't change human nature," is false. It is false because it is precisely the ability to change that distinguishes human nature from all other aspects of nature. Nature's cycles repeat endlessly, and animals do not change because their instinctual life suffices to guide, protect, and continue their species. Within the processes of evolution, changes of course occur, but these require vast periods of time and do not compare with what we are discussing here. Man closely resembles the animals in possessing an instinctual nature or something like instincts. This is necessary to say because for some years psychologists have been trying to upgrade the concept of instinct by calling it "need," "urge," "drive," or even "erg." Whatever the name, these are powerful influences, particularly when heightened by glandular secretions. Most healthy people are aware of the effects of fear or anger in stimulating the adrenal glands, which in turn so affect the body that one can in instances even feel the hair raise on the nape of the neck like that of a frightened or enraged animal.

Students approaching an examination hour or an employee asking for a raise in salary often demonstrate the effects of excess adrenalin which can be said to prepare one for fight or flight. Since neither fight nor flight will solve the immediate problem—however an irritated student would like to pummel the professor—the wise teacher sometimes can radically diminish the effects of excess adrenalin by making a joking reference to the physiological processes taking place in most of his students. The power of adrenalin to hasten the heartbeat, increase respiration, add sugar to the blood (e.g., the release of glycogen from the liver), which adds to one's capacity for fight or flight, is known to most students, and a reference to these matters calms the anxieties and enables persons to settle down and do their best in the examination. What is more important here is that control of the "adrenal syndrome" by rational processes demonstrates that man can control to a significant extent the influences of his instinctual nature, even where this nature is reinforced chemically by the powerful secretions of ductless glands like the adrenal.

In the search for identity and maturity one might suspect that the branches of the psychological sciences that deal with personality would offer a great deal of help. Disappointment awaits the seeker here, for there is no unified theory and little agreement among the specialists in this field. Theories of personality abound by the score, many of them by world-famous psychologists and psychiatrists. The scientific and practical values of these theories have not percolated down to the common man, who might conceivably profit from the investigations of the specialists. Far too many people view personality as a sort of jigsaw puzzle that somehow must be put together. The accomplishment of the task presumably makes one a complete, mature person. But as one advances upon the task, the pieces just do not fit together and some seem to be missing entirely. As a result the picture is never completed. It follows that it is better to look at man, as personality or a self, as an organism, an organization. It is better still to look at man as unique, a product of nature to be sure, but still different from everything else in nature. This difference is seen in man's capacity to stand above nature and to judge and evaluate nature, to find fault with it and to improve upon it. But it is precisely this capacity of man, his uniqueness, that raises trouble as far as science is concerned. Science is not interested in the unique but in the general. The task of science is to reduce knowledge to general laws, and by definition it is not interested in the exceptions, the unique elements. It takes notice of the exceptions, the biological "sports," but only in passing.

A science of man would seem to be a contradiction in terms. Yet that is what we are seeking in our understanding of man. How to be scientific and yet pay attention to what is central in man's makeup, his uniqueness, poses a real problem. To study man scientifically is to reduce him to the status of a thing, an object to be manipulated as one necessarily manipulates the other objects that science measures. Carl Rogers has written movingly on the problems involved in treating persons scientifically and the dangers involved in the procedure. The economic, sociological, and political implication of such treatment are enough to give nightmares to a sensitive person. Aldous Huxley's *Brave New World* would be a paradise in comparison to the managed society resulting from a completely scientific handling of personality. One preview of this sort of thing is found in George Orwell's book *1984*. One of the difficulties of the personality sciences has been their dependence upon the physical and biological sciences for terminology. Instead of coining fresh new terms and concepts descriptive of man's actions, attitudes, aptitudes, and aspirations, psychologists and sociologists have been content to borrow from other more exciting, more exact sciences. We take "ergs" and "drives" from physics, "homeostasis" from biology. "Valence," so important in Kurt Lewin's theory of personality, is borrowed from chemistry, and "data-processing," equally important now in describing man's logical capacities (why not call them that?), is on loan from the omniscient computers. The engineers also get into the act and "human engineering" (unhappy phrase) describes certain aspects of personnel work. The list could be extended, but enough has been said to point out the fact that man increasingly is seen and treated as a machine that is to be oiled, adjusted, tinkered with as any other object, in order that it may operate at full efficiency. In contrast to this trend we assert the primacy of the person. Man is a person with a destiny, not a machine to be used and then discarded when worn or outdated.

The aim of all psychological measurement, and indeed an aim of all the behavioral sciences, is predictability. While in certain limited areas, such as vocational choice and intellectual capacity, this aim is helpful and justifiable in assisting people to make right choices, should absolute predictability ever be attained, the end result could be a managed, stultified society where man at last was reduced to the status of mere animal whose needs and urges could be anticipated, managed, and met. The elite who presumably would do the managing eventually would fall prey to the same forces that brutalized the ordinary man, and civilization as we know it would cease. This thought will be elaborated later on. Fortunately this pessimistic picture will probably never be developed from the photographer's negative. The reason is that man, conscious or unconscious of his uniqueness, refuses to be treated as an animal or as a thing. As these words are being written, Negroes in Mississippi and other states are asserting their right to be treated as men, as citizens, as human beings. This right is denied them by a minority of misguided people who have little knowledge of or interest in the personality sciences, but who yet are exemplifying one of the dangerous tendencies of those same sciences. Ignore man in his uniqueness, treat him as an animal or a machine, and you will destroy society and civilization as we have known it.

One of the ironies of present-day American life is that we are involved in an operation in Vietnam dedicated to ensure the survival of democratic institutions in that area of the world (only recently acquainted with democracy), while at the same time hundreds of thousands of our own citizens in America are denied some of the most elemental rights of democracy. It is quite obvious that the question: "What is man?" is far from being rhetorical. It is one of the most practical questions that faces us today. Who am I? What am I to become? What am I headed for? How am I to achieve my potentialities?—these are some of the most important questions of the moment, and they are significant questions for all men. To treat a segment of our population as subhuman, to deny them rights enjoyed by the majority, is to filter out of humanity some of its most important ingredients. Of these, self-knowledge, or self-understanding, is most vital.

One of San Francisco's authors and newspaper columnists, Herb Caen, has been quoted as saying: "The world's biggest problems today are really infinitesimal: the atom, the ovum, and a bit of pigment." The threat of atomic destruction and the threat of population explosion are more than matched by the racial tensions that hang over America and indeed over the entire world like a Kansas tornado. Rudyard Kipling's plaint about "the white man's burden" is a caricature in view of the emergence of China as a world power. One who really knows what it is to be human, to be a man, to be a person, achieves maturity not by denigrating his fellowman, but by personal involvement in helping his fellowman to attain his own potentialities. One who is on the road to maturity knows the compassionate truth of Eugene Debs's words: "Where there is hunger, I am not fed. Where there is a soul in prison, I am not free."

There are many influences both within ourselves and in our environment that militate against a genuine understanding of one's self. Of these only a few have been mentioned: the individualism that is so important to Western culture which has built fantastic mechanical and social means of communication in the midst of a rising tide of *human* loneliness, isolation, and alienation. The pervasive force of various types of determinism was touched upon as one of the causes of the modern malaise, and this compounds the difficulties in the third factor, that of motivation. If a person has been marked by a corrosive home-life as a child, where can he find strength of motivation for change? Psychiatrists report that increasing numbers of patients reflect the influence of developmental psychology by explaining their problems as the result of the lack of maternal love or of paternal weakness. Earlier the specialists were plagued by patients who reflected Adler's psychology and accounted for their problems in terms of inferiority complexes. Perhaps tomorrow's patient will complain of being deprived of LSD in the formulative period of his youth.

That people have problems is quite obvious. But to view man as a problem to be solved, which statistical experts at least infer, is to make a tragic detour. Man is not a problem but a potential person who needs to grow and develop and find meaning in his personal existence. The significance of goals, of purpose, of the use of present and future time, are seen by increasing numbers of people in the "helping professions" as being profoundly determinative precisely because they are not deterministic, for the person himself becomes motivated to make his own choices, real decisions whereby he himself determines what he is to become.

4

THE ISOLATED SELF

NEAR THE CITY of San Rafael in California is located an unusual school: Guide Dogs for the Blind. Here dogs are bred from the finest breeding stock that has been developed over twenty years of intensive research. They live in kennels on the campus of the school. We all are aware of the fact that psychological tests as well as other tests are used in our public schools. At this particular school the students are tested too, by skilled specialists who check the dogs on intelligence, keen senses, willingness to work, and evenness of temperament. This testing goes on weekly from the day the puppies are seven weeks old until they reach thirteen weeks.

At thirteen weeks of age the future guide dogs destined to provide sight for the blind are farmed out to selected youngsters—members of the nationally known 4-H clubs of farm children. Here they live for a full year and are taught simple obedience. Why this particular phase of the project? The answer to this question brings us to the heart of what we want to discuss in this chapter. The answer is simply this: it has been found that dogs need the love and affection of a normal home in order to develop the kind of character or "identity" that makes a good guide dog. Here is established scientific fact or truth from animal psychology that underlines our basic human need for love more pertinently than those interesting observations gleaned from laboratory rats and their mazes, their shocked behavior, and their resultant learning. The quality of love that we receive from infancy on to adolescence determines to a great extent both our capacity to give and to receive love, and the ability to arrive at an emotionally secure adult life.

The isolated person usually is loveless, for he is both unloved and unloving. At the least he feels unloved and shows little capacity for loving others. If he has had no abiding experience of love, he is unable to recognize its varied forms or he perceives it as a caricature. When love or concern is offered as in the acceptance of a skilled psychotherapist, the neurotic or psychotic patient for a long period of time may resist, reject, or view it with suspicion. It is a language he has yet to learn to speak and, accordingly, he distrusts those who use it. Like an infant with no vocabulary, he has to begin to learn by the tone of voice, facial expression, gestures, and the discipline or dependability of the adults around him.

Recently a girl of sixteen was admitted to a large California state hospital for the mentally retarded. That she should be in such an institution seemed adequately demonstrated by the fact that her intelligence tests showed a score of 50, about half of what is considered to be normal or average mental ability. After a thorough study had been made of her record, the word went out that she was to be treated with firmness, but also with kindness and patience, regardless of what she did. For three months Sue screamed, scratched, bit, and kicked her way around the hospital with no retaliation except restraint when she became too violent or abusive. She was not ignored or merely tolerated but was treated with mature love. Then a remarkable thing happened: Apparently convinced of the genuineness of the attitude of the adults around her, she relaxed and her aggressive personality made a 180 degree turn. She became comparatively gentle and began applying herself to her school work. Within a few weeks a second testing by the psychologists showed her intelligence quotient score to be 130.

A person's intelligence is not raised 80 points merely by being exposed to mature love. The girl described above had the same intelligence when she entered the hospital as she had when she was retested. The secret of the change was felt to be due to the considerate treatment she received apparently for the first time in her entire life. Abandoned by her father before she was born, and by her mother shortly after birth, she had been farmed out to disinterested relatives. Then followed a series of foster parents more interested in the money they received for her support than in giving her a bit of love. A history of running away and other escapades showed her to be far more familiar with juvenile court and detention hall than with anything approaching a normal home environment. Deprived of love from infancy, she never developed the basic trust that Erikson speaks of and she distrusted the actions and motives of adults and of her peers alike. The surprising thing was the relatively short time it took to bring out the more positive aspects of her personality.

The capacity and need of the infant for love is practically infinite. This is the burden of the message we get today from our specialists in child study and care. When I was a teen-ager I felt suffused with measureless wisdom as I instructed my long-suffering eldest sister on how to raise and treat her infant sons. Filled with pride at my new title of "uncle," I went along with the popular folklore and spoke sagely about "spoiling children" and about the danger of too much gentleness resulting in "spoiled brats." One day the oldest nephew, having arrived at a husky six years, kicked me on the shin after one of my lectures. I predicted darkly and angrily that those boys would come to no good end. One is now a very successful physician; one is a skilled aeronautical engineer; and the third, a popular high school teacher. Here, to paraphrase Paul, the "foolishness" of patient parental love was wiser than the "wisdom" of those afraid of "spoiling" the child.

It follows that to spoil an infant or a child by showering him with adequate love is impossible. The world to the tiny infant is one big blooming confusion of light, color, sound, chatter, and an environment suited primarily for the convenience of adults. Lewis Sherrill has suggested the imaginative experiment of placing oneself in the world of the tiny child. Here one is imprisoned in a place where ceilings are miles high, chairs and other furniture sized to fit giants, doorknobs out of reach, and so on. Add to this the mystery of unknown language, of sounds, of activities that are incomprehensible except for the few pleasures of cuddling, sucking, cleanliness, dangling baubles, and sleep. If fear and anxiety of the unknown are powerful forces to the adult with rational ability, to what extent do they influence the small child whose logical capacities are undeveloped? The love of emotionally adequate parents is a powerful antidote to the fearful and confusing aspects of the environment of the child.

Unhappily, the impatient adolescent idea of spoiling children is not absent from the modern scene. Not long ago a young father came to me with a very distressing problem. His wife's parents were visiting, but this was no humor-evoking mother-in-law situation. He reported that the grandparents would slap his infant child forcefully about the head for messy table manners. The child, fed in a high chair, was just beginning to learn to manipulate a spoon. The father felt that the grandparents were extreme in their idea of discipline, but lacked the courage to assert himself in defense of his own baby. That this is not an isolated instance can be proved by the daily edition of any metropolitan newspaper. With monotonous regularity it is reported how inadequate parents act out and work out their own personal frustrations, anger, and aggression on their helpless children.

A social worker recently reported to me her experience with a child in a local private school for disturbed children. The child's face was scarred like that of a long-time second-rate prize fighter. The scars came from beatings administered by the child's father, who used his own leather belt, buckle end down. This child's chief administrative offense was running away to San Francisco, eighteen miles distant. So skilled was he that he could draw a map of the city's transportation system to show the social worker how he did it. His purpose in running away was to get back to the home from which the children's court had removed him for his own protection in order to get what shreds of love and security he could receive there. The child was nine years old.

Where love is adequately experienced by the infant in the

first year or two of his life, the result is a tremendous foundation stone for the total personality, for he has already developed an ability to trust. The psychiatrist Erik Erikson has stressed this fact in a series of books that treat the developmental crises of life. The seven stages of life that Shakespeare delineated are amplified by Erikson into eight. Of these, three seem to be of paramount importance for modern man in his search for maturity. In infancy one learns either an attitude of trust or basic mistrust of people and of one's own environment. In adolescence one either achieves identity or suffers from identity diffusion. In mature age one arrives at integrity or faces the rapidly diminishing future with despair.

The achievement of trust can come about in spite of the most appalling social conditions. A friend of mine who works among the Puerto Rican slums of New York City speaks of an "under the roof" feeling that loving parents are able to inculcate in their children. Overcrowded, subdivided apartments shared by several families would seem inevitably to provide only one-way tickets to Sing Sing prison. The opposite is true of many individuals born "on the wrong side of the tracks," who are known to all of us. The answer seems to lie in the quality of love that they have received and the resultant trust with which they have faced their world and their responsibilities.

Max Lerner holds that slums and poverty are pathetic but not tragic. Tragedy has deeper, often mysterious, causes, but the pathetic elements of life stem from human conditions that man can change. In a moving description of his immigrant family and its poverty in the slums of New York City, Lerner tells how the cohesiveness of the family, with resultant support and love, built lasting values. The strong masculine image of the father as head of the house is a product of the more authoritarian European culture, but it had migrated to America along with the family. In the father-and-son relationship of the immigrant family Lerner finds a parallel in the pioneer period of American history. Here father and son worked together carving a new life out of the wilderness, and in that era the son had far fewer difficulties in achieving his identity.

In America we customarily deride the authoritarian aspect of European and Oriental family life, even though that appears to be changing rapidly. One significant value in these differing cultures is that the young adolescent with an adequately masculine figure in the home does have a relationship conducive to forming an adequate identity for himself. If the authority is too harsh, he at least has a strong figure to rebel against and thus is not a "rebel without cause." It is no mystery why the search for identity seems so frantic for so many modern youth. Our philosophers and psychologists have indicated many reasons why the modern youth has so much difficulty in achieving identity. One significant cause is that we have replaced the authoritarian home with the permissive home, and the price we are paying for our freedom from authority is high in terms of instability, delinquency, neuroticism, and lack of meaning in many lives. The extremely permissive home is actually frightening to the small child who occasionally is naughty just to see if the parents will set the limits that he needs and unconsciously desires. The older child has similar needs and is baffled when these are not met. The permissive home is dismaying to the adolescent who seeks guidance (most of all when resisting it). With father absent and hard at work building family financial security, and too tired to build lines of communication with his son when he is home, the problem is obvious. But where the father definitely does not appear manly, adequate, and mature, and when he evades the son's attempts to communicate or is embarrassed by them, how can the son trust his father?

Lacking an adequate source of identity in parents and consequently not trusting their parents, modern adolescents seek trust in their own peer groups, the gang, the club, the concomitant thrill of trying the forbidden in alcohol, sex, and drugs. They speedily find themselves allied against the "they" of parents, teachers, policemen, and society in general. It is as though the adolescents are saying, "If I cannot find an adequate source of identity, I at least know what I ought not to be, and so I'll be that!" The hair grows, unkempt and uncut, the smile becomes a sneer, the walk becomes a swagger, girls are objects to be used and discarded, home is a place to sleep, ambition and work are mere jokes. One of the end points is, of course, state prison and here completely alienated inmates find their only source of identity in the contradictory consolation that everybody on the outside is a square.

In a large California prison a short time ago a group of specialists concentrated on the record of one inmate in order to understand all they could about him. Correctional officers, psychologists, teachers, chaplain, psychiatrist, and others all reported on many hours of interviews and counseling. This man had attempted to rob a busy supermarket under conditions that practically guaranteed his capture before he left the store. "For the first time in my life I felt like a man when I held that gun in my hand," he stated in an interview. One may smile at the apt phallic symbolism of the gun which Freud pointed out long ago. The symbolism indicates quite accurately the dignity, identity, adequacy, and sense of worth that had been denied this man. Here was no dangerous criminal, nor even an adult delinquent. What he really did was to make a feeble, if dangerous, protest against the deprivation and emasculation brought about by his familial, educational, social, economic, and marital failures.

The juvenile delinquent is deserted, anxious, scared, angry, and retaliatory. This is the summation of J. M. Stubblebine, psychiatrist, consultant, and Program Chief of Community Mental Health Services of San Francisco. Since the juvenile delinquent sees or experiences his environment as threatening, he attempts to cope with it by behavior that is largely defensive, or full of defenses. Hence the exaggerated swagger, the dress, the switchblade knife, which amplifies one's strength while the true self inside remains scared. By being deserted, Dr. Stubblebine means that the emotional needs of the adolescent remain unmet, whether or not his parents actually desert him.

I have a friend who operates a psychiatric clinic for the disturbed children of his area. He complained bitterly one day that most of his patients were children from wealthy homes in the community. "Their mothers are so busy with do-gooder auxiliary work raising money for sweet charity that they have no time for their own homes and children." Such children have opulent homes, a high degree of material security, ponies, cars, attend summer camps, but can be lacking in the emotional security, the love, the genuine communication and relationship that every developing human requires to become mature, or to have an "identity." Lewis Sherrill has reminded us that people who are not able to give of themselves give *things* to their children. And the children know the difference! Let this not add to the guilt of concerned parents who also like to give toys on occasion to their children. The toy given along with the self, the interest, and love of the parents is, of course, a good thing. The toy, or car, or European trip given to *avoid* personal involvement becomes a bad thing. The stress on love here again requires the clarification that parental love is not indulgence or mere permissiveness. Love (as I have stated elsewhere) has a full spectrum of many colors, and the colors here stressed are discipline and constancy in dealing with the needs of children, for they may become delinquent or disturbed when these factors are missing from their daily experience.

What seems to be paramount in the emphasis of many different approaches to human problems is the necessity of mature love mediated to the child. This message comes through from psychologists, social workers, psychiatrists, medical doctors, probation officers, ministers, and counselors. Where genuine love and understanding are lacking, it follows that a person is unable to learn to trust other people and his environment. Lack of trust seems to have a stockpiling effect—one of the cumulative effects in human experience. He who cannot trust his parents cannot learn to trust his fellowman, and most important of all he cannot even trust himself. He misses his own appointment with destiny—his identity; and in losing identity, he can also lose health and mental stability. Delinquency, crime, alcoholism, marital failure, mental and physical breakdown can be the results.

It does not follow from the above discussion that I am pleading for a sticky "togetherness" of the sentimental type where the parents are omnipresent in all the affairs of the child. The child needs and deserves a privacy, his own autonomy and initiative, as Erikson puts it, which parents should respect. Too much togetherness can drive a child to rebellion faster than any other cause—this is a mistake that "sophisticated" parents often make. Tournier in his inimitable way describes delightfully how a child makes a great step forward in achieving selfhood, or early identity. This comes about when he has a secret. To whom shall he confide his secret? To his mother or to his best friend? The great moment comes when the child decides to carry out one of the first cuttings of the psychological umbilical cord and tells the secret to his friend. The parent who is hurt or annoyed at this stage of the child's development has not learned that weaning applies to parents quite as much as to the child. He has not learned that the child, at every stage of development, has a right to a separate existence.

I shall never forget a young woman who was referred by her doctor for counseling. For years she had suffered the domination of perfectionist, demanding parents until she was afraid to live her own life. She had married a classmate, who was a considerate and understanding husband, and they were deeply in love. Yet the birth of her first baby, a fine healthy infant, left her with a depression that required a few months' hospitalization in a mental health clinic. She was swept with feelings of hopelessness, with feelings of inability to measure up to the demands of motherhood now added to the duties of wife and housekeeper. Perfectionism invariably is a symptom of deep-seated anxiety over one's capacities to perform adequately on the stage of life. Or it might be said to be a result of the dominance of the child that remains within every adult. After months of counseling, this patient one day said with a faraway sound to her voice, "Only now do I begin to feel like a separate person." I felt like a midwife at the birth of a healthy new baby!

The infant needs to be weaned from the breast or the bottle

to more solid foods. The small child needs to be weaned from the protection of parents and home to later childhood and its adventures. The older child needs to be weaned to adolescence, and most of us spend the rest of our lives being weaned from the querulous demands and torments of adolescence to true maturity. But the parent also needs to go through a similar process of weaning. The parent must appreciate and accept the day when the infant stands on his own feet and begins to explore the world. I have known mothers to indulge in baby talk to the extent that their child was able to communicate with utterly no one except mama, with whom he had his private language. When school age is reached, then the speech therapist has to be sent for—all because *mama* was not *weaned* from her baby.

Parents need to be weaned from overprotective attitudes as the older child enters adolescence. The child proceeding toward adulthood has to assert himself if he is to find identity, and here a certain amount of rebellion is healthy and inevitable. Parents become anvils upon which the adolescent occasionally pounds out his ideas. This is more painful to parents than to anvils, but precisely here is where a person is called upon to be adult. The parent who cannot take an occasional aggressive attack without counterattack demonstrates anxiety rather than maturity. How can children develop psychological and emotional muscles if they cannot try them out from time to time? The adult parent can take a small child's aggressive attack: "I'll kill you, I hate you!" with a smile and a calm statement: "We all feel that way sometimes." The anxious parent is shocked and retorts: "God will send you to Hell if you don't love Mommy," and the resultant neurotic guilt and its repression may take $5,000 worth of psychoanalysis to overcome it years later.

The final step of parental weaning comes when the adolescent is ready to accept responsibilities of adulthood, of vocation, and of the establishment of his own family. A great temptation for many parents is to hover protectively over the new nest, something that even birds have sense enough not to do. Herein lies the source of so many unnecessary "in-law" problems. The father who can grasp his son's hand and welcome him sincerely into the world of responsible adulthood, man-to-man, is truly adult. From here on in his son is no longer his dependent and inferior child, but his equal and his friend. One of the saddest things for the psychologist to witness in life and in therapy is the picture of a father who is jealous or feels inferior over the actual or possible achievements of his son. It is as possible for parents and adult children to establish a genuine relationship as friends on a basis of equality as it is possible for married couples to be friends as well as lovers, but it is comparatively rare in our culture.

The emphasis in this chapter so far has been upon the necessity of adequate love, resultant trust, and dependable relationships upon which identity can be based. What about the adult in search of maturity who feels rightly or wrongly that he can detect deficiencies in these matters in his own familial and psychological development? Far too many parents for that matter suffer far too much neurotic guilt for their failures as they read "magazine psychology" and identify mistakes or faulty attitudes toward their children. Gordon Allport has reminded us that if genuine love is present in the parents' attitudes, this love will get through to the child, though he may not be aware of it until he himself reaches maturity. But what of the adult who feels isolated and lacking in a strong identity because of actual deprivation in his developmental years? To repeat the words of Nicodemus: "How can a man be born when he is old? Can he enter a second time into his mother's womb and be born?" The answer he received was, "You must be born anew."

Much of modern psychology and particularly psychotherapy seems to underline the answer that Nicodemus received. To be born anew is to recognize one's capacities for decision as an adult. The adult strives to be objective and recognizes with Nietzsche that "in every man there is hidden a child that wants to play." He can learn that the child within him has fears and anxieties related to the incomprehensible world of the small child. But now he is an adult who has far more resources with which to cope with his child-world, and the fear or anxiety that it induced. Becoming more objective, the adult who seeks a shortcut to maturity will recognize values of the child that are worth retaining—his imaginativeness, his creativity, and his joy at the newness and beauty in his world. We also have underrated the terrific perceptive capacity of the small child, some of which we can regain if we relax as adults. I think of an eight-year-old girl patiently waiting to be recognized by an imperious woman presiding over a table of baubles at a rummage sale. The child had a dime in one hand and a bit of costume jewelry in the other. Finally the woman deigned to notice her and said impatiently: "What do you want? That costs a dime." Silently the child handed up her dime and as she turned away I heard her mutter to herself, "Children also are people." Martin Buber states that the gift of the Spirit is awareness, and the adult who so desires still can achieve this gift as well as the perceptive child, for whom it seems such a natural endowment. If the adult person does not have awareness, then a usual substitution is that of "bewareness" as he views with suspicious eyes his world and his fellows as threatening, untrustworthy, and even dangerous.

If love is vital to the small infant, it is still more vital to the love-starved adult world. Psychotherapy of all types seeks to utilize and implement love as a therapeutic tool. Erich Fromm holds that unless one gains or regains a capacity for love, only superficial changes can be accomplished in therapy. In a recent psychosomatic clinic of which I am a member, a surgeon presented a patient about whose request and need for additional surgery he had serious doubts. The interviewing psychiatrist gently and skillfully brought out the facts that here was a woman, lonely, depressed, without meaning or purpose in life, whose chief problem was what Frankl has styled existential frustration. For her, life seemed so empty that surgery meant a few days in the hospital where she had care, attention, and at least some significance to others around her. In his summary after the patient was dismissed from the interview the psychiatrist said, "This patient needs, more than anything else, the milk of human kindness." The adult who would lessen his own isolation can experiment with giving mature love in the form of simple human kindness to other more needy people, and he might be startled by the results.

Trust that has been stressed as significant in the developing life of the infant can also be recovered by the adult who desires it. Trust is more than a tiny child's naïve acceptance of his parents' dependability and the recognition of his environment as trustworthy. This is a more or less unconscious factor in the child's experience. Trust can also be a consciously chosen adult attitude, the result of a rational choice to be tried out and lived by experimentally. It is my conviction that man has the capacity to escape the straitjacket of past experience, heredity, and environment. He is rather a "becoming," an emerging person. We are human *becomings* rather than human *beings*. Identity ultimately is not the result of a desperate search. We all have identity. We *are* identities. The question for adolescent and adult alike should not be and really is not, "Who am I?" but more responsibly, "What am I now and who do I want to become?" Identity then is not seen as a fixed goal, a frozen state of the personality however ideal, but an ongoing process richly rewarding because of continually unfolding and exciting new vistas of possible accomplishment.

5

THE DIVIDED SELF

AN ASTUTE STUDENT of human nature in the nineteenth century and one who anticipated some of the psychological ferment of the twentieth century was Nathaniel Hawthorne. In his book *The Scarlet Letter,* published several years before the birth of Sigmund Freud, Hawthorne gave an explicit and vivid description of unconscious processes that decades later were to be subjected to scientific scrutiny by Freud. It is these unconscious processes, labeled the id by Freudian psychoanalysts, that are a significant source of the phoniness in human nature and human relationships discussed in the preceding chapter. Hawthorne's prescription for phoniness is not unlike that of Sidney Jourard's insistence upon honest self-disclosure to at least one other significant person. "Be true! Be true! Be true! Show freely to the world if not your worst, yet some trait whereby the worst may be inferred." So urges Hawthorne in his concern for genuine dealings between people who have the possibility of becoming genuine persons. His demand is not unlike that of Nietzsche, the brooding German philosopher, who makes a similar point in saying that before man can become more good he must become more evil. The intention here is that a person must recognize the evil in himself before the potential good can become an effective force in his life. This is the secret of human existence which in one way or another was learned by the saints of both Christian and non-Christian religions, who were well aware of dark forces in and the powers of the unconscious states of our being.

Another way of posing the problem is to ask the question,

"What is your concept of Man?" Or to put it more directly, "What is a human being?" Modern thought seems to be ambivalent here, for it sees man as something between an animal and a computing machine. Modern culture is increasingly manipulative as huge computers take over tasks heretofore performed by people. Man becomes a number on a card, and his fate or career can be vitally affected by the calculations that the machine inexorably grinds out. As a result, man is treated sometimes as an animal, with needs such as sex drives, and sometimes as a machine, with input and output geared to the efficiency of the Organization of which he is a part. Less and less is man treated as a rational person or as a Self, with certain and infinite potentialities for growth. A manipulative culture seeks to control his growth and sets limits on this growth for the ultimate good of the greater machine, the Organization, the Corporation, the Institution—these things which rebellious youth today lump together under the term "Establishment."

Paralleling the twin phenomena of the apathy of some youth, and the violent demonstrations of others in their efforts to confront the Establishment, is the quiet despair, the experience of loneliness, the feeling of emptiness, and the alienation of men and women caught up within the power and influence of the Establishment. They cannot defy, demonstrate, or drop out. There are very few middle-aged Gauguins around today! There is the mortgage, the children's education, the retirement security to consider. There is so much that seems phony in the whole business of living as well as in earning a living. No one is more aware of this than the counselor striving to help a sensitive client who often is repelled by the ethics of business practices deemed necessary to get ahead. Even in Russia it is reported that psychotherapists are diagnosing a new illness: "party-functionary neurosis." This is suffered in men whose inner nature rebels against carrying out orders of the Party that violate their sense of decency and morality.

There is a real gulf between human aspirations and human limitations. There are some real differences between what a man is and what he would like to become. Self-assessment would seem to be a vital resource in facing the predicament that life presents to so many people today. Blaming one's failures, problems, frustrations on the outer world, on the Establishment, is understandably human and often true. It is also the child's reaction or defense, and that of the adult who is "other-directed" instead of "inner-directed." Viktor Frankl, in his writings as well as in his personal experience points up repeatedly that the most appalling circumstances of life can be alleviated and even overcome by the attitude with which one faces them. He has quite adequately demonstrated that man can transcend, surmount, very real strictures that either heredity or environment, or both, can place upon his life. Most significant at this juncture is the attitude with which a person faces his own real self. Much in the inner self is unlovely and unlovable, and we so desperately want to be loved, to be significant, to others. Much inside us is fearful and fearing, hateful and hated, weak and childish, murderous rage and unbridled lust. Freud was right in calling this unconscious part of the self a "seething chaos." H. G. Wells styled it "the civil war within the self." Our dim awareness of the inner turmoil arouses what Kierkegaard called "Dread" and what we moderns know as "Anxiety."

The Roman stoic Seneca was well aware of the power of anxiety over men's lives. "Nothing is terrible in things except fear itself," he wrote, reminding men that the object of fear is fear itself. In America's early involvement in World War II, President Roosevelt went on the air with his statement of Seneca's wisdom: "The only thing we have to fear is fear itself." Fear always has a specific object. Anxiety is often defined as "free-floating," without a specific object. We are anxious about things in the depths of our being that are not "nice" and "good." We repress them as Freud says because they seem so terrible, so threatening. But powerful desires and drives are demonic, as Tillich puts it. Oblivious of the repression, they bubble in the witch's caldron of the inner self, and the steam rises as anxiety. This anxiety tries to help us by putting dreadful and sometimes superficially polite masks on all men, on all things, and events. The superpatriot sees a mask of the international Communist on everyone who does not subscribe to his own narrow brand of "true Americanism." The mental patient, struggling with his deep hostility, puts the masks of plotter and hater on everyone. The enemy is everyone, and everyone is set to destroy him. When things don't go our way (and how often do they really?), we put on the mask of the hurt child and complain: "I'm a born loser. I never get the breaks." In most interpersonal relationships, masks, I suppose, are necessary and often useful. The The very word "person" comes from the Latin *persona,* meaning "mask." Tournier discusses this in his writings, but he prefers the term "personage" to "mask." I have a small boy's irresponsible sense of humor with regard to women's hats. But long ago I learned in the interests of domestic tranquillity to "repress" it, and find something safely appreciative to say. This is, I insist, a legitimate use of the mask. Another such use comes into play when you call on a friend who is convalescing from serious illness. He is definitely on the road to recovery but still looks ghastly. The Puritan ethic of "honesty" requires you to say as do the Germans: "Man, you look like *Todt auf Urlaub*" (Death on a vacation). But you just don't say that. You don the mask of jovial friendship and say: "You look great —I'm happy you're coming out of it so well." But if the friend is dying of cancer (why do the obituaries evade the word and say, "After long illness"?), to put on a jovial, hail-fellow-well-met mask is simple cruelty. Now is the time, as Viktor Frankl urges, to drop masks, be genuine, and address ourselves to the meaning of life, of suffering, of death, and our attitudes toward these.

Masks are protective, and at times are honestly useful, particularly in our relationships with other people. But if we don them as we seek to understand ourselves, we are doubly deluded. We do not fool others, who usually are quite discerning in detecting the phony, and we do not fool ourselves, for the end product in our experience is guilt compounded with more anxiety. But apparently one of the greatest problems facing modern man is fear of taking an honest look at himself. Abraham H. Maslov has written movingly and poignantly on the fear of knowledge, the evasion of knowledge, the pains and dangers of knowing our real selves. According to him: "*The great cause of much psychological illness is the fear of knowledge of oneself—of one's emotions, impulses, memories, capacities, potentialities, of one's destiny.*" The frightened, confused child, who early has received some hard blows, sometimes shows a lot of apathy. This apathy is a response to anxiety and is a way of avoiding knowledge. The adult also can avoid knowing, can avoid the knowledge he needs to reduce his anxiety. The woman who fears to consult the doctor after finding a lump in her breast is anxious and afraid the diagnosis may be cancer. Here fear of knowledge often enough is fatal. Knowledge of the truth can set her free of morbid anxiety, and diagnosis can set in motion the means of treatment, usually after surgery has ascertained the truth about the lump—whether it is malignant or benign. The Scriptural injunction: "You will know the truth and the truth will make you free" is not only superb preventive medicine but it remains an excellent prescription for physical and mental health. Knowledge of anything carries with it responsibility and the necessity of making decisions, responsible decisions based on the knowledge gained.

We shrink from knowledge not only because it demands the work of decision-making but also because it is so normal to fear anything that might make us appear weak, bad, inferior—these things that might tear down our self-esteem or minimize the persons we like to think we are. This is seen very clearly in psychotherapy where a problem may be stated by the client in the first interview. Then ensue weeks of "sparring," called by the psychoanalytical term of "resistance." This is our defensive behavior in which we attempt to ward off the therapist's efforts to help us to see the whole truth about ourselves. Sometimes a person comes for help, but is so distrustful of the therapist, and so fearful of disclosing his inner life, that weeks go by before he can honestly bring up the real problem that drove him to seek therapy. Another form of devious behavior whereby we try to hide the actual self is the device of coming for help for a specific problem of a "friend" who is too shy to seek therapy. I learned about this from my very first client in psychotherapy in a large university. She was troubled about a girl friend who was a Lesbian, a homosexual. After a few consultations in which she learned to trust our relationship, the problem shifted into first person, without the girl's ever apparently noticing it. This particular phenomenon in psychotherapy is more rare today, perhaps because Freud and Kinsey have taught people to be less shy on sexual matters.

The attempt to reduce the high voltage of anxiety without using a transformer is bound to fail. The transformer is, of course, an honest look at the self. Here again another difficulty is seen. Not only do we find it painful to look at our area of limitation where we are afraid to appear worthless, but we also avoid knowledge of our basic capacities and potentialities. It is my conviction that a great many people are neurotic today, and the neuroses are caused by the fact that their talents, their unique potentialities, have not been used. They are "spinning their wheels" in life because they have not grown as they could have grown, because they have not used the gifts they have, and their energy has not been thrown into the proper gear. Morton Hunt has researched a massive volume *Her Infinite Variety,* which discusses the problem of intelligent women who "have everything" but somehow are still ill at ease with life. The solution is to put into motion constructive work—in community, in the arts, in business—that will utilize the untapped resources of creative women. Many a psychotherapist has been alert enough to see in a so-called neurotic client a person whose anxiety is traceable to the fact that he has not utilized the creativity within himself. As the counseling focuses upon creativity and the true meaning of vocation as a significant focus of one's capacities, the neurotic symptoms drop like unneeded spectacles from the eyes as the client proceeds to become happily involved in creative work. Anxiety arises then from our fear of facing our limitations and from our fear of facing our potentialities. Our human dilemma involves or arises from the fact that at one and the same time we feel inferior and superior. We fear both the inadequacy shown up in our limitations and the demand for responsible decisions required by our potentialities. We lack the "courage to be," as Tillich entitled one of his books. Courage to face real limitations and to recognize them as a real part of one's self, and courage to face the challenge of one's potentialities, is one thing we all can use. One of the psalms asks, "What is man, that thou art mindful of him?" The translators of the venerable King James Version of the Bible lacked courage to translate the answer accurately. The answer to the question is: "Thou hast created him little lower than 'Elohim.' " The word "Elohim" was translated as "the angels." The accurate translation is "God." "Thou hast created him little lower than God." Here again is a deeply psychological affirmation about the truth of man's existence. He, it is true, has his childish weaknesses, inferiorities, and so on, but he also has his godlike capacities even though he may shrink from the responsibilities that these call forth.

Man's capacity to transcend himself, to rise above very real limitations of heredity and environment, is one of the basic emphases of the existentialist philosophers and psychotherapists. As Viktor Frankl has reminded us, it is true that we have instincts but it is not necessarily true that the instincts *have us!* We can control instinctual drives by a responsible use of our capacity to make decisions. Instinct pushes for an immediate gratification of desire. This is where the animal and the child are similar, as countless experiments have demonstrated. But the unique human capacity is that which enables the adult to postpone immediate gratification of desire in the interest of greater fulfillment. The need for sexual satisfaction along with the need for intimacy and relationship accounts for many early marriages which founder all too soon on the rocks of divorce. This tragedy results from our fear of knowing what our real needs, our real goals, and our potentialities are. Unable to face self-knowledge, self-examination, we rush into temporary solutions. Unable to chart a course because we are ignorant of all the possibilities present we sail into what seems a safe harbor—such as early marriage—only to learn that it is too shallow for safe anchorage in the storms that are pending.

It is man's capacity to transcend himself, which means the ability to get outside himself for an honest look at what he is, that offers the secret to the solution of the human dilemma. The human dilemma that I am concerned with here is our judgment of ourselves as worms along with the feeling, at times at least, that we can perform as gods. If we are created "little lower than God," there is no need for apologizing for the daring creativity that lurks within men. It seeks expression, and if denied expression, gives us our troubles and neuroses. If we focus on the worm aspect of the dilemma, we are defeated before we start to live. Erich Fromm has put the point succinctly: "So many people die before they really begin to live." Heidegger, the German philosopher, has suggested that man's nature—his "lower" and his "higher," his creatureliness and his godlikeness, his negative and his positive—is a basic part of our humanness. This he calls "dividedness" and this is a permanent part of our being, of our human existence as differentiated from all other animals. Animals do not experience this division, they cannot stand off and judge themselves as "good" or "bad," "weak" or "strong." In a moving passage in the novel *Five Smooth Stones,* Gramp describes the rare situation in terms of the jungle. The lion, king of beasts, lives off the weak, because "he's got them all scared." The grandson agrees but insists that it is only half true. The lion doesn't *know,* as he feeds on a freshly killed antelope, that other antelopes could get together and trample him to death in five minutes. "Hell of it is," the grandson concludes, "the antelope doesn't know it either."

The difference between the jungle of nature and the jungle and ghetto of Western culture lies in our knowing what the lion and the antelope cannot know, our uneasy knowledge that things can be and should be different. It is neither a good thing nor a bad thing that we are divided. It is just the way things are; man has to deal with this as a permanent part of his make-up. It is what makes him superior to animals, it is what makes him the "lord of creation," naming the beasts as is described in the Genesis myth of paradise. The psychiatrist Ludwig Le-Febre argues that not only is man divided at every step of the way, but that only as such is he truly human! Animals, in sharp contrast, are whole, fitting neatly and completely into the natural scheme of things. Man, like animals, arises from nature but he dares to stand erect in judgment of nature. He feels himself divided from nature and compelled to control nature rather than submit supinely as animals must. We cannot escape suffering, separation, anxiety, and death as the negative experiences of life. The animal does not resist death, as does man. When it senses the approach of death, the animal seeks a place in a thicket to die quietly. Man's resistance to illness and death spurred medical science so that our life expectancy has doubled and redoubled since the medieval period of history.

Heidegger's contribution to our understanding of man as the being who always is divided can be likened to the outrigger canoe, part of which is separated from the main part. The specimens of these canoes that I have seen in the South Pacific often are beautifully shaped and carved. The outrigger, often enough, is a simple log, sometimes with stubs of branches showing. The canoe is beautiful and the outrigger is not. But without the outrigger the canoe will capsize in the surf. Man in denying to himself some of his negative feelings, experiences, and actions is denying a very real and necessary part of himself—his outrigger, as it were. When he pretends that he is only a handsome canoe, presenting a plausible front to the world, and attempts to assure himself that this is his whole being, his integrity is off-balance and his life is in danger of capsizing.

The existentialist writers, of whom Heidegger is a leader, have taught us that man can "be himself" and also can be away from himself, or not himself precisely because he is divided. Martin Buber teaches a similar truth in his classic book *I and Thou*. The baby comes to awareness of himself only after he has experienced "other selves" in the world about him. Before the awareness of himself as a separate being, he has been "away from himself." As a small child, after some stupid action on my part, I found that while running I could lift a heel high enough to kick myself as punishment for my stupidity. Much later I recalled this type of behavior and wondered which part of myself stood off and judged it necessary to punish another part of myself. Viktor Frankl in a more serious vein points out that the man who condemns himself as utterly worthless possesses in this very judgment of himself the dignity of a judge. In psychotherapy this insight into man's divided nature can become the turning point, the "critical incident" wherein a despairing client begins to take faltering steps toward recovery.

Not to be oneself, to be away from oneself, is often quite a normal experience. Many an exasperated wife can testify to this as she repeatedly calls a usually lusty eater to dinner. Her call falls on deaf ears because her star boarder is not himself. He is away from himself, absorbed in polishing his golf clubs, tinkering with the hi-fi, or absorbed in the latest issue of *Playboy*. The eminent psychologist William James gave a final lecture at Harvard on the day that he retired. A colleague saw him looking very gloomy and reassured him that retirement was not all that bad. James brightened and said: "I am looking forward eagerly to retirement. It is just that I always am terrified before a class of students and I dread giving this last lecture." Urbane, sophisticated, and very learned, James was well aware of his shy, fearing "not-self" that did not show on the platform. Once I was requested by a very able and popular public speaker to give him psychological tests. He assured me he was very introverted, but I disagreed, reminding him of how much at ease he seemed as a speaker and in social life. However, the tests showed a very high degree of introversion. The public self of this man was quite different from the inner self. The shy introvert temperament is not a negative thing as many introverts seem to assume. It can be surmounted as in the case of James and of the public speaker, and it can be channeled into an intuitive awareness and sensitivity to others' needs and feelings.

Deeply committed lovers are quite aware of dividedness. Love and hate are opposites. One cannot exist without the other. One day a wife was very angry with her husband. When she became silent he said: "My Mickie loves me very much. Otherwise she could not get so angry with me." Hawthorne observed: "It is a curious subject of observation and inquiry whether hatred and love be not the same thing at bottom. Each, in its utmost development, supposes a high degree of intimacy and heart knowledge; each renders one individual dependent for the food of his affections and spiritual life upon another; each leaves the passionate lover or the no less passionate hater forlorn and desolate by the withdrawal of his subjects." He is describing the old physician, Roger Chillingworth, who intensely hated Arthur Dimmesdale, the minister. When Arthur died, Roger's life, deprived of the object of his hatred, seemed to become increasingly meaningless and shortly thereafter he too died.

I have tried to show that dividedness is an accurate way of perceiving ourselves. Thanks to nature's invention of sex, Le-Febre states, "there is no such thing as 'man'; there are female and male human beings." As a Frenchman might put it, *Vive la différence!* Negative and positive are not necessarily separated into "good" and "bad." Illness, for example, is not "always bad." With some people it has been the beginning point and goad to great creativity. The biography of many literary and artistic people abundantly illustrates this fact. Illness can also serve notice that a way of life which produced it must be changed. Is death really bad? Our knowledge that we must die creates within us what Tillich has styled "the anxiety of finitude" or "existential anxiety," because our existence is threatened by impending death. Viktor Frankl asks if death, after all, does not belong to life, as the ending does to a story. Heidegger and other existentialists maintain that unless man comes to terms with death he cannot begin to live. Important for self-understanding, self-actualization, and a viable method of escaping phoniness is to see that dividedness cannot be escaped through denial, repression, or masks. These can lead eventually only into the maze of meaninglessness, the labyrinth of loneliness where it is difficult to find Ariadne's cord. In the healthy person dividedness is integrated into his ongoing living. The fear of knowing can be transmuted into the fear of *not* knowing the truth about ourselves. Fear is then not a negative attitude but one with a positive function.

Man is a creature, but a creature with infinite aspirations. Reinhold Niebuhr in his monumental work *The Nature and Destiny of Man* describes man as "a spirit who stands outside of nature, life, and himself, his reason and the world." Our nature then is twofold with a "higher" and a "lower." Abraham Maslow feels that "most philosophies and religions, Eastern as well as Western have dichotomized body and spirit, teaching that the way to become 'higher' is to renounce and master the 'lower.' " The existentialists, however, teach that *both* are simultaneously defining characteristics of human nature. Neither can be repudiated without doing violence to man; they can only be integrated. An objective study of the struggles of a Paul and a Martin Luther and a Pope concerned about birth control shows the futility of renouncing the "lower" in the attempt to deny its proper place as part of our nature. If we face the "lower" in all honesty, it loses its power to contribute to our anxiety and guilt. Nothing could be "lower" than death, the final ironic experience that divides us from family, friends, the world, and life itself—death, which asks for our identity and which Sartre calls absurd. But men can face death and consequently find more profound meaning in life.

Man can know life and himself most completely only by grasping the prickly nettle of negative experience. The prickle is not really painful to the adult who takes a firm hold on all the experiences of life, not merely the pleasant ones. We can't all be Zorba the Greek, but we can share more of his zest for living. The first chapter in Carl Rogers' book *On Becoming a Person* is entitled "This Is Me." In it Rogers gives an honest self-appraisal, an account of his life, background, education, motivations, activities, and goals. His example seems to be an excellent way to make a beginning in "disclosing man to himself." The problem of identity is never solved by wondering or wailing over it. Its recurrent question: "Who am I?" has a specific answer: "This is me." The answer poses another question: "What do I want to become?" for as Scheler, Sartre, and others teach, man decides what he is becoming—he makes himself. Take another look at the outrigger of your personal canoe, a long hard look, and then be glad it's there!

6

THE CONFLICTED SELF

A CAPABLE MAN of decision is universally admired for his ability to make good judgments and to act accordingly. Sages and philosophers of all cultures, primitive and sophisticated, have described him and praised his virtues in myth and in prose. Across the centuries and the continents, from Confucius to Cicero, there is a basic agreement on the essential elements of a person with integrity. The wise man is a decisive man of character and dependability. He has integrated the negative aspects of his self so that they do not clash with but serve to strengthen the positive factors of his being. He has learned to regroup his forces like a wise military commander after a temporary setback. Fear of failure is integrated through rational examination of possible causes of failure into a fear of not achieving his goal. The difference may seem slight, but it is a watershed that divides the decisive personality from the conflicted. Longfellow has portrayed both types of being in these words: "We judge ourselves by what we feel capable of doing, while others judge us by what we have already done." Here is the familiar dichotomy of the man we think we are and the man that others know we are.

The comparison of the decisive personality with our own achievements often is a depressing matter. Deciding between two or more alternatives automatically produces conflict that usually is painful. A South American friend tells me of a man who was marked by extreme indecision. A bequest left him the choice of one of two valuable properties: oil land in Oklahoma or a ranch in Brazil. After months of agony he chose the ranch in Brazil. His ranch manager told him to choose between beans and cotton, the two most marketable crops. While he tarried in his choice, boll weevils multiplied and promptly devoured the cotton he finally decided to plant. The following year delay in deciding for the beans resulted in a drought that destroyed the crop. In despair he traded his ranch for a small but flourishing airline. High over the Andes in the executive plane, his pilot turned to say: "Sorry, sir, engine trouble. Choose a parachute, because we'll have to bail out." Anxiety speeded this decision. He donned the parachute, jumped, pulled the ring, but the parachute failed to open. Being a devout man, he fervently prayed: "O St. Francis, save me." From a nearby cloud came a clear voice: "St Francis Assisi, or St. Francis Xavier?"

The conflicted person easily and perhaps grimly recognizes how this story bears upon his problem. Inability to make decisions, the "wavering to and fro," can have disastrous consequences. The problem is a personal one, of course, but the recurring crises of the second half of the twentieth century show it to be social, national, and indeed international. James Russell Lowell lines it out for our generation: "Once to every man and nation Comes the moment to decide, In the strife of truth with falsehood, For the good or evil side." Despite the solemn music to which these words were put, I used to rebel against the "once only" element. Now I have learned that the poetic insight of Lowell is trenchantly demonstrated in history and in the tragic social, racial, and military crises of the present hour. The call to decision inevitably arouses conflict in a man who must decide. We who continually are deciding what we are becoming can affect not only our own growth and self-development but also, in significant decisions, the destiny of others. The responsibility inherent in deciding heightens the intensity of the conflict that a person feels within himself.

The existence of and experience of conflict is not the reprehensible or abnormal thing that so many people seem to feel, as though they must apologize for its existence in themselves. Conflict is not abnormal. It is one of the most normal and frequent experiences any vital person can have. What is abnormal about the matter is the ways, the extraordinarily devious ways we follow in order to avoid conflict, the necessity of dealing with it. One of the most familiar of these is that of postponement: "Tomorrow will be a better day." Sometimes people try to live by this sort of postponing the inevitable day of decision. In the novel *Gone with the Wind*, Scarlett O'Hara spent most of her entire life postponing the vital decisions of life because "tomorrow is another day." More serious than postponement (after all, there is the possibility that one *will* decide tomorrow) is that of regression or retreating into a simpler but safer mode of existence. Another method of handling conflict is to stand still, to "block," as psychology styles it. A third reaction tempts the wavering one to detour around the horrendous involvement that the conflict suggests is necessary before he can decide. The last and healthy action is to move boldly ahead into the threatening possibilities of the encounter that lies ahead. These ways of responding are sketched below. The symbol "X" represents the problem, or conflict, calling for decision. The arrowed lines depict the common ways men act to solve the problem.

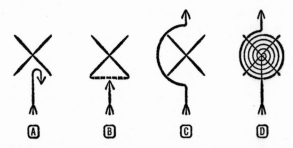

Figure A shows the pattern of the individual who regresses. He is the true child of Otto Rank's birth trauma theory. His solution to the problem of enemy attack is quite simple: Retreat! (Military history is filled with generals of dubious ability who were well acquainted with this solution.) The child of Rank's psychology says to himself: "Back to the womb. Back to a simpler and safer way of existence where decisions are made for me." The psychotherapist sees this child not infrequently. When the regression becomes extreme it is called pathological and the individual victim of retreat needs special treatment and at times hospital care. The issue of regression from conflict is seen not only in offices of the psychotherapists but in many areas of life. Men of demonstrated ability have been known to refuse promotions because of inner insecurity and doubt of their ability to face necessary conflict and make correct decisions. Today many corporations indulge in a quiet and often desperate search for junior executives who are willing to exercise responsibility, to risk the dangers of wrong decisions.

The individual who is appalled by the challenge of conflict and who "blocks" or stands still (Figure B) does not retreat or regress, but neither does he advance any farther to meet the demands of life. I think of a highly talented musician and organist, a friend of my college days. After one year of college he went home never to return to school. He was so attached to home and mother that he could not endure the prospect of separation. The college authorities enlarged the music department and asked me to invite my friend to come to teach pipe organ. His reply to my urging was, "I like it here in the home town, and anyway, music doesn't challenge me anymore." His considerable musical talent was never utilized as he remained content in a small business and safe at home.

The third type of evasion is more subtle (Figure C). The person who adopts the procedure of detouring around the conflict often is well above average in intelligence. He uses his intelligence not in productive ways but to devise sneaky detours around the conflict with its demands for decision, commitment, and action. While teaching in a university, I became well acquainted with a charming young man of this type. We shared committee work on intramural affairs of the school and his ideas were numerous and helpful. But his academic work was appalling. One day I called him into my office and proceeded to berate him for his academic record. He was hurt, and defended himself: "I haven't flunked a single course." "Precisely," was my rejoinder. "If you would flunk, we could dismiss you, but you use your high intelligence to do the minimal amount of work to get by. You could be at the top of your class." Thereupon he smiled smugly and said, "My teacher in sixth grade told me I was a genius." I had given his class the psychological tests for intelligence, and so I replied: "She was right, but you haven't done an honest day's work since. You use your high intelligence to discover the minimum work necessary to get by." The temptation to detour is quite prevalent. All of us have known it and at times have tried it. Nietzsche again comes to mind: "Hidden in all of us is the child who wants to play." Life requires the child to grow into the man, and if he lets detouring become a lifetime practice or habit, he never will grow up. He will be followed all his life by a ghost. The name of the ghost is, "The man you might have been."

There remains but one more direction for action. This is to tackle the conflict head on, squarely, in spite of its threat and potential hurt or even defeat. Figure D thus is intended to resemble the way the cartoonist depicts a fight. A man investigating a noise in a dark room may find a burglar or just the cat that his wife forgot to put out. The noise, with its unknown possibilities, may make a child hide his head under the covers hoping the noise will go away. The man must investigate, for the unknown presents more terrors than the known. If it is a burglar and our man is beaten and robbed, well, as Robert Burns has it, "A man's a man for a' that!" If it is just the cat, there is quiet satisfaction for the man that he had the courage to face the unknown and its possible dangers. Conflict that is honestly engaged in provides one with valuable experience regardless of the possible outcome of success or defeat. Even the negative factor of failing to handle the conflict adequately leaves one with the fact that he did make a valiant attempt and did not evade, run away, or shrink back from responsibility. Most of us find that we learn more from our failures than from our too easy successes which can breed a brash overconfidence.

Conflict, like tension, is a very real and pervasive part of day-to-day living. Without tension drumheads go soggy, as in humid weather, and the beat is late. Without tension the fiddle string slips out of pitch and the melody is flat. Avoidance of conflict sometimes seems to the child to be the only way to relate to a domineering parent. I know a man approaching middle age (whenever that is) who is still tied to a successful but forceful and autocratic father. A mutual friend said of him, "When that man's father dies he really is going to start to live or else he will go all to pieces." He apparently repressed all normal adolescent rebellion and self-assertion in his anxiety to avoid conflict. An indication of this is frequent, almost violent reaction to his peers when they are in the role of an authority figure. It does not follow that this type of interaction is true of all successful autocratic fathers and their sons.

Domineering people often can use their influence in ways that result creatively. It is reliably reported that the well-known architect Frank Lloyd Wright had a most indomitable mother who decided before Frank was conceived that: (1) She would have a baby. (2) It would be a boy. (3) He would be a genius. (4) He would be the world's greatest architect. Now, to have a baby is easy for a wife to decide. To decide that the baby would be a boy is quite another thing and a matter that the science of genetics has not yet quite caught up with. But then Mrs. Wright was a resolute woman! The architect was accused by many who knew him, including near relatives, of insufferable egotism. Such egotism is quite understandable in one who was told from infancy that he was to be an architect, and that he was to be the best. Erik Erikson's developmental stages of autonomy and initiative are recalled when we learn that crayon designs and toy block patterns Wright made at the age of seven still were being repeated in his architectural designs seventy years later. His mother hung geometric "mobiles" over his crib and provided him with the largest of toy building blocks. I have repeated Nietzsche on the child in the man, but Eric Berne in his *Transactional Analysis in Psychotherapy* reminds us that the child not only is playful but also highly imaginative, perceptive, and creative.

The self-confidence of Frank Lloyd Wright is revealed in

the story of his first visit to Tokyo. Here he found that the
Japanese had antedated some of his advanced architectural ideas
by a few hundred years. When questioned about this he replied, "I merely find my ideas confirmed here." The man interests me not only in his fascinating psychological effervescence
but also because his last creation before his death was the
County Center Building in the county in which I have my
home. During the first rain after dedication it leaked like a
sieve—a Wright trademark which he joked about to complain-
ing people for whom he had designed homes. But the building
is easily the most interesting in the county and immediately
became a tourist attraction. What I think follows from all this
is that creativity can be encouraged through a constructive use
of conflict. An overpowering mother and a strong-willed son
undoubtedly came into collision many times. Conflicts involv-
ing other people, or controversial issues, and conflicts arising
within the self can be destructive of human values, but they
also can be channeled into artistic and scientific achievement.

A man who was so disturbed mentally and emotionally that
he felt himself to be possessed by demons is described in the
Bible. He came to Jesus, who went straight to the heart of the
man's difficulty with the apparently disarming question: "What
is your name?" The reply confirmed Jesus' implicit diagnosis
of the difficulty: "My name is Legion." To this day chaotic,
fearful forces within a self, the anxiety, aggression, and guilt
buried deep inside, can tear a person apart into what seems
like many persons. The man whom Jesus addressed clearly was
not a unified person, an organized self, not a self-actualized,
integrated personality, a mature adult sure of his identity—
or whatever other descriptive term you prefer. His name was
Legion, many names, divided into many persons, or more
accurately, segments of a person. And this man is but an extreme example of the definite measure of control that inner and
often unconscious forces have over our lives.

No one is completely unified, organized, adjusted, integrated,
actualized, or mature. Though we certainly are Being—human
beings—let us not forget the thrill and incitement of the fact

which the existentialists affirm: We are always Becoming: Our potential self is *not* a fixed thing like a rock that the elements slowly wear away, or an immutable law that permits no change.

That's why "to be Normal" is nothing to brag about, as Dr. William Pemberton has insisted. The completely normal person would be so dead-center average that he could not communicate with the rest of us. Dr. Louis Bisch frankly says, "Be glad you're neurotic," in his book of that title. He reminds the reader that creativity is not divorced from neurosis and that the job is to winnow out disturbing neurotic traits while keeping the valuable ones. An eccentric but lovable guy can either become an alcoholic or a great writer. Jack London accomplished both goals!

The chaotic, inner forces that produce conflict, anxiety, and guilt are located by Freud in what he calls the id, the unconscious state of man's being. I locate the source of our temptation to play the phony in what Jung calls "the dark shadow," and it was exquisitely described by Hawthorne in *The Scarlet Letter* in 1850. And before Hawthorne, The Psalms, The Book of Job, and Paul discuss this in poignant language. In addition to the inner turmoil, there are environmental forces outside us —both friendly and hostile—that struggle for domination of our lives, our Being. Today we are at a sort of crossroads in the discussion as to the relative strength and power over us of these two sets of forces. A debate is current in all behavioral sciences such as psychology, sociology, psychiatry, anthropology: Is man helpless and driven by unconscious factors of which he is unaware, or can he somehow control these and with his rational conscious mind have energy enough to cope with the outside problems that fly at us from the breakfast table until bedtime?

Freud has rightly emphasized the tremendous amounts of energy that we consume just in suppressing antisocial thoughts, desires, and impulses which spring so speedily from the id. At the breakfast table it must be decided whether the sixteen-year-old son with a new driver's license gets the car that evening. Father has indigestion, which doesn't help the discussion, but worse, buried in his unconscious are a dozen scenes with his own irritable, arbitrary, forceful but, even so, sometimes lovable father whom he hated, feared, and sometimes liked. This ancestor is whispering into his unconscious ear: "Keep kids in their place. Grown-ups come first. Kids should be seen and not heard. Why, in *my* day . . ." But what is his rational mind saying to the boy? "I'd like you to have the car, but Saturday traffic is too dangerous, and I hear those dances have been pretty wild." Mother feels that the boy should have the car and says so emphatically. The real cause of her emotion is that she gave up dancing when she married Father, who was brought up in a cult that taught that dancing was a sin. She has always resented this, but in supporting her son's plea for the car a part of herself is saying to Dad, "Why don't you take *me* out once in a while?"

On the way to his office the car radio announces gloomy news that depresses the stock market. This stirs up deep feelings of insecurity in Papa that he has never faced. Perhaps they are too deep to dredge up—the little boy despairing over his ever-failing efforts to meet his father's perfectionist demands. Actually he is a very successful corporation executive. On arrival at the office he is all primed to jump on Casper Milquetoast for an error that later in the day he discovers he himself had made. Victims of his frustration are not confined to the office. The error he made caused loss of a valuable contract. His usually very capable secretary is at home sick, though he suspects a hangover, for he well knows her weaknesses! At four o'clock his most capable junior executive announces that he has accepted a flattering offer from a rival firm. On the way home his Cadillac rams the car ahead at a stop light all because he was grimly enjoying a fantasy in which he was throttling his secretary and his junior executive. On arrival home the slam of the door is a prelude to a scene that takes little imagination to describe.

Posing the personal problem the more sharply is the fact that today our world itself tends to be chaotic, insecure, disorganized, with sharply opposed ideologies in our country and in other lands. No one knows this better than the high school senior who is caught on the horns of not one but several dilemmas. Get a job? Try to get into college? Join the military force? Loaf and wait for the draft? Defy the draft via demonstration? Go to Canada to start a new life? These issues recur continually in the counselor's office. The sensitive high school senior sees the extraordinary achievements of science focused primarily on human destruction instead of on human welfare. His own scientific and social education in high school in many cases is superior to the learning his father received in college. He is aware that 60 percent of the national budget of his and of many other countries is devoted to "defense." Small wonder that his natural idealism is blunted into cynicism, apathy, or the selfish desire to "get mine." The conflicts of society, nation, and world are shoved relentlessly at him with the ruthless demand to decide *now*.

More than at any other period of history, circumstances today call on us as individuals, communities, and nations to be integrated at the highest and best levels of personality organization. The present world is for adults only! But there is more than a suspicion that world tension and conflict are only the inner struggle of the self, magnified and projected onto the world. Many thoughtful men have seen this. Professor Eric Jaensch, of the University of Marburg, long before World War II stated: "The basic problem between nations is not economic, social, or political, but psychological." He insisted that if men cannot, or will not, seek to understand one another's attitudes, motives, fears, and capacities, that if we will not communicate honestly, we will continue to have tragic consequences. Examples enough fill the sadder pages of history. Kaiser Wilhelm of Germany in 1914 renounced a treaty guaranteeing the neutrality of Belgium. His troops invaded Belgium and world opinion mobilized against Germany. The American "Exclusion Act" of 1924 excluded all but a very few Japanese from entering America. This was an unnecessary slap on a sensitive face which was returned with interest at Pearl Harbor in 1941. Von Ribbentrop,

Hitler's ambassador to England, was socially snubbed by the British, who could not forget that earlier he had been a mere wine salesman in England before Hitler's era. Furious at the British, von Ribbentrop assured Hitler that England would not come to the support of the French when Hitler started World War II. These three items from history demonstrate that the ignoring of the psychological milieu—needs, anxieties, emotions of nations as well as of individuals—can spell disaster. The American Foreign Aid Program is an attempt at meeting this situation, and the Peace Corps and hospital ship tours are worthy examples of meeting desperate needs. But our national dichotomy diverts untold resources, human and material, into the tragedy of Vietnam that has caused worldwide concern.

It is so human to seek to evade the conflict in life with its pressures for decision. Like trapped animals we run from corner to corner seeking an easy way out. Our evasion can become pathological and make us sick. Amnesia, disassociation of personality (*The Three Faces of Eve*), and schizophrenia (splitting off from reality and living in a fantasy world) are some of the extreme and more desperate attempts to adjust to the world, to handle our conflict, anxiety, and guilt. They are attempts, "escape hatches," to withdraw from the day-to-day living which often brings painful experience that we try to avoid. Psychotherapy of all types tries to help a person face the realities of today, the possibilities of the future, and regain confidence that he can handle tasks that life presents.

Let us now take a look at the anxiety that pervades our lives and yet paradoxically makes us more human. Something akin to anticipatory anxiety can be seen in animals, but that which you and I share is uniquely human. One of the interesting theories of the origin of anxiety is that of Otto Rank, an early disciple of Freud. Rank points out that our intrauterine existence, nine months of peace in the womb, is obviously blissful. This womb life is free from all conflicts of any kind, particularly those of a psychical nature. The act of being born represents a radical upheaval, producing a psychic shock of great consequence. The resultant traumatic separation from the mother is one to which the individual never is reconciled, and herein lies the source of his anxiety.

Some have felt that one proof of Rank's theory is the way some patients in mental hospitals withdraw from reality. They do not speak or move, but wrap their arms around their knees in a "fetal" position for hours at a time. At this stage of regression the patient sometimes is called "catatonic." The story is told of a noted psychiatrist who, when showing visitors through his hospital, came upon such a patient all folded up like an unborn baby. "This," he said, "is a catatonic. The world is too harsh for him and he has regressed until he feels he is safe, back in the womb." The visitors moved on to the next ward. The mute, catatonic patient looked up at the ward attendant, and speaking for the first time in months, he said, "Did you ever hear such damfool nonsense?" The conclusion of the story has it that the patient was shortly thereafter discharged. Gordon Allport, in one of his papers, made a plea for a return to common sense in psychology, and this patient very likely would agree enthusiastically.

Freud agreed that the act of birth is our first experience attended by anxiety but felt that Rank overemphasized the business. After all, the baby has no knowledge of any danger at birth, and can only sense the exciting disturbance in his environment. Here you are in a warm, comfortable place, suspended in a sort of hammock, surrounded by liquid (hydraulic shock absorber, as it were)! It is dark, fairly quiet. There is an automatic food service and a disposal system with no diapers, discipline, or decision, no conflict, anxiety, or guilt. Suddenly, birth: harsh light; cold air you must gasp to learn to breathe maybe with the assistance of a slap on your bottom; grasping hands; uncomfortable clothing; automatic food service permanently disconnected. Now you must cry and work, suck to get food. Maybe Rank is right for those few individuals who find life "outside" just too difficult, and they may carry a lifelong resentment at being born. Could this also be a possible psychological explanation of the fascination that nudism presents to some folk, the desire to return to simple womb life where clothes are unneeded?

My reaction to Rank's theory was first theological and then humorous. How could the Creator be so stupid as to blast the race with anxiety by making it the inevitable outcome of the only possible process by which we arrive into the world? Such stupidity is matched only by those moderns who view sexual intercourse—the prelude to their very existence—with a sense of shame and guilt. Humor reminds us that Rank committed that twofold error so easily perpetrated in psychology: assigning impressive names to mysterious phenomena as though this explains them (schizophrenia!), and using too simple a hypothesis to account for too many profound, unknown factors. Ferenczi, an early associate of Freud, in diametric contrast to the Rankian theory, said, "The more I observe, the more I realize that none of the developments and changes which life brings finds the individual so well prepared for as birth." To him birth is "an agreeable and triumphant transition for the infant." I am sure all obstetricians, gynecologists, and pediatricians agree with Ferenczi, for of the many of my acquaintances I do not know one who is not happy and enthusiastic about his work of assisting life to come into being and to grow.

The well-known theologian Paul Tillich finds the source of our anxiety in our very finitude, our knowledge that we are finite and here for a temporary stay and must eventually die. Man of all the animals knows anxiety, for he alone knows that he must die. But this knowledge is man's greatness also. The animal knows neither anxiety, freedom, nor the conflict of decision because he is driven by deep instincts that decide for him. Man does have something like instinct, but he has more: a freedom and ability to make choices between real alternatives. We are finite, we know that our days are numbered and we resist. We would prefer to be like God: infinite, no limitations on us or on what we want to do. How the wise men have teased us on this! Bertrand Russell: "All men would like to be God and some few of us refuse to admit the impossibility"; Oliver Wendell Holmes: "The first step toward true

faith and true religion is to admit at least that *I* am not *God*";
Wilhelm Reich: "Most intellectual people do not believe in God,
but they fear him just the same." I think that Reich speaks for
many moderns, who, though able to dismiss God from their
concerns, find it impossible to dismiss anxiety and guilt, despite
frantic efforts that seem only to increase their neurosis.

The Freudians tell us of the omnipotent feelings of the infant:
he cries and is fed; he calls and is attended to and entertained;
like God, he has all power, he is omnipotent, he is the center of
attention, the center of the world, but it is a very small world
and he must immediately start the learning of that fact. His
philosophy is, to quote a line from Victor Herbert's operetta:
"I want what I want when I want it!" People who keep this
philosophy into adulthood are in trouble, for the world refuses
to give them the privileges of the infant. The infantile feeling
of omnipotence so helpfully discussed in the writings of Erik
Erikson is not confined to the infant stage of life, because the
child remains within us. It may be called the psychological
equivalent of the theological teaching on sin. Many devout
people are confused here in pluralizing the word into "sins."
There are many "transgressions" in our lives, but there is only
one Sin. It is not "committed"; it is an attitude of defiance
based on self-centeredness. Sin is egocentricity, the placing of
self in the center of the universe, a position fit only for God.
Sin is self-service as contrasted to the serving of others. Paul
succinctly defines sin as worshiping and serving the creature
rather than the Creator. In Greek the word "sin" means "missing the mark." In a seminar with psychiatrists interested in
what theology teaches about man, this Greek definition was
immediately related by the therapists to the problem of neurosis. Erich Fromm has an interesting thought that connects
his rejection of Rank's theory with the fact of sin. In a recent
lecture he argued that man does not wish to return to the idyllic
life of the womb, but rather to the cave. The cave is Fromm's
symbol of a simpler mode of existence—easy, childlike, and free
from duty and responsibility. This desire he calls the Original
Sin of man.

The anxiety of finitude (which Tillich also calls existential anxiety, because our existence is threatened and limited) can be integrated into our lives so that it need not cripple us, enervate us, and make us hopeless, as it does so many neurotic people. The way to integrate and to control anxiety is to choose a viable attitude that helps us face the fact that life is transient. If we have a linear view, if we look at our lives as a line (as long a line as possible, of course), no matter how far we can see along the line, or walk along it, it will stop or eventually be broken. In this view, which is time-centered, longevity is eagerly and desperately sought after. No one has delineated more poignantly this view of finitude than the pessimistic author of Ecclesiastes: "Before the silver cord is snapped, or the golden bowl is broken, or the pitcher is broken at the fountain, or the wheel broken at the cistern, and the dust returns to the earth as it was . . ."

A better way to visualize life is with two lines making a V, with birth signified by the base of the symbol. Now the transitoriness of life can be viewed as "the expanding universe" of the microcosm, of the self, of *me*. Transitoriness now becomes opportunity to fill the expanding V with as much constructive living, loving, working, playing, serving, and worshiping (if your God is not dead!) as is possible. Of course, at some time a horizontal force is going to shear the V, and this is death. Whether your V continues on to infinity despite the shear depends upon your concept of eternity. We can be eternity-minded as well as time-minded. Eternity for me signifies quality of living, and time symbolizes quantity or length of life. Viktor Frankl states that transitoriness is a reminder to be responsible. "After all," he says, "if we were immortal, we would put off necessary tasks until tomorrow. We would be 'Mañana' people." Finitude and its anxiety now can be utilized by making worthy choices, wise decisions, and using the freedom and time given us for responsible living. Erikson's chart of the life cycle of man ends with the crisis of old age, wherein one has gained integrity, or lives by despair. This correlates with my comparison of the linear view with the V idea of life. One looking along a line that is to be snapped sooner or later is tempted to despair. The "V for victory" was used by Winston Churchill to ward off foreboding fears of defeat and to galvanize his whole nation. It is not beyond the range of the possible that it can do the same for the individual self.

A substantial problem in the conflicted self is guilt, a late arrival in the developing life, for it is preceded by anxiety, frustration, and aggression. Responsibility and guilt characterize all human existence. They go together like Siamese twins, for if we are not responsible, we could not be guilty. Guilt arises from malignancy in human relationships. It is the cancer that destroys the good cells of love and life much like the tottering characters in *Who's Afraid of Virginia Woolf?* hacked away at one another's selves, while yet leaning on and desperately needing one another. Guilt arises from our moral failures, from our ethical failures (there's a difference!), from our sin, our "missing the mark," of the goals we seek, or *should* seek. This guilt is called "real," or "actual," or "normal," or (that word again!) "existential" guilt.

Judeo-Christian religion in its Biblical emphasis makes it quite clear what this is all about. Normal guilt, as I shall call it, results from violation of the laws of society, or of God, or when one fails in a commitment. I chose the word "normal" as an adjective for guilt because that's the way things are! If you run a stop sign with your car, you are guilty. It is that simple—no matter (and I agree with you) that many stop signs seem idiotically placed. Your offense, and guilt, are greater if in running the stop sign, you crash into and damage another car. Such guilt can and should subside after forgiveness, restitution, and meeting of possible legal penalties. Guilt is usually felt as it is proportionate to the offense. Running a stop sign and its consequences often arouse more anger or annoyance than guilt. The point I am making turns on the legal factor. When one fails in a commitment as did Conrad's Lord Jim, who as captain deserted a sinking ship loaded with terrified passengers, guilt becomes a thing that can dominate all of one's life, as it did that of Lord Jim. All his life long he was followed by the re-membrance and by his feelings of unworth.

Man's guilt belongs to and is an important part of the di-videdness that I discussed earlier. To return for a moment to the idea of man as an outrigger canoe: the outrigger stands for the negative parts of one's self that a person would like to forget, overlook, or deny. Not all negative things are "bad," but we can view them as bad, wishing that they were otherwise. The introvert may envy the extrovert. The brunet may prefer to be blond; the girl may wish she were a boy (as some men wish they were women). Before I got used to my nose, I envied my fellowman's whenever it was straighter! In all men guilt rides heavy on the outrigger, and too much weight here endangers, or may capsize, the whole affair. This is precisely what happens in the forms of emotional or mental distress called neurosis and psychosis. Guilt that is not incorporated, included, or integrated can endanger a person and make him neurotic. A heavy burden of guilt that one cannot handle can capsize the life, and psycho-sis results. The solution is to transfer the guilt from the out-rigger into the heart of the craft—to admit it, not repress it. This is what Tillich means by "the courage to be." Too often a person lacks courage to be his real self, his whole self, nega-tive and positive. To accept himself as he really is is to see that humanity would not be humanity without its frail side, its sin, its guilt. To be aware of normal guilt and its self-condemnation is to take them honestly as part of the self. This puts a person farther along the road of self-understanding, and far beyond the one who denies or rationalizes away his negative nature. A most important conclusion here is that normal guilt always is a conscious experience. The normal man ought to feel or to be aware of normal guilt, for it is a permanent part of human existence.

Neurotic guilt causes a great deal of difficulty because we are unaware of its origin, and because it works in such devious ways. Tillich says, "The moralistic self-defense of the neurotic makes him see guilt where there is no guilt or where one is guilty only in a very indirect way." Many case histories give abundant evidence of this. For example, a man sent the post office a check for thirty-seven cents to pay for the use of a two-cent stamp a second time many years before. He had carefully calculated the compound interest on two cents. The neurotic mother unconsciously rejects her child. His birth interfered with her social plans. Guilt at the rejection is so horrible to admit that it is repressed into the unconscious and comes out as extreme fussiness and overprotective attitudes toward the child. The same dynamics operate from the standpoint of the child. It is normal for the child to be aggressive at least at times. But if his scream of "I hate you" is answered by parental threat of withdrawal of love, this is so frightening to the child that his aggression usually is repressed. Years later it emerges as vague feelings of unworth, or as a habit of outwitting people of authority. So what? What is wrong with admitting that I didn't want this or that child? Children can be monsters, who interfere with our plans, as well as dolls ready to give more love than they receive!

Fathers should also come in for their share of attention at this point. Most male psychologists like to focus upon the weakness of the mother! One of my students once worked with a family in which he called the father "the arm-breaker." This was because the father deliberately broke his son's arm while beating him. The boy was an exceptional student of whom the father was intensely jealous because of his own deep feelings of inadequacy. His rage at himself and his own weaknesses was not faced but projected upon the boy.

Parents may not like this, but in the interests of minimizing neurotic (and unnecessary) guilt they need to be, and should be, more like God to small children. The infant and the child have no concept of God. They do know love, tenderness, patience, dependability, joy, and comfort. These all are "God words," found in the Bible, but they also are ways of relating to small and often anxious children. Parents are physically larger and usually more emotionally mature than their children. They should be able to face aggressive attacks, "unreasonable" outbursts, of frightened and insecure children without reacting in the same manner. Long before psychiatrists discovered the values of emotional "catharsis," the prophets and writers of the psalms were advocating and practicing it. To be Godlike in the family is not primarily to be pious or even devout, but, above all, understanding, compassionate, and accepting of the child's frustration and aggression as well as his love. First things first!

What I call the "sin of invidious comparison" of siblings often leads to neurotic guilt. Jim, a very capable professional man, from his earliest memories was always compared to a bright older brother, who eventually became a corporation president. Jim's parents in his case no doubt had the best of intentions in goading him with reminders of his brother's ability and success in school. The brighter the brother shone, the more they too might glow in reflected light. The end result, however, is that Jim, though successful in many ways, continues to remain deeply insecure, feeling inadequate and somehow guilty. The habit of blaming oneself, other people, or an unkind fate is another sample of neurotic guilt. Everyone knows some part of this, for it too is part of humanity, of our dividedness. The extremely neurotic person lives in a very real hell of self-judgment. He suffers from malnutrition of his own humanity and is crippled by an incapacity either to receive love or to give it.

This chapter has focused upon the almost daily problems of conflicts that call for decisions that often are so difficult to make. Our anxiety and guilt compound the difficulty, but they are as much a part of us as our complexion and our heartbeat. Where indicated, psychotherapy offers healing in terms of a relationship of warmth, understanding, and acceptance. Ideally the therapist sees you primarily as a person, not as a problem or as a bundle of difficulties. But Gordon Allport cogently remarks that psychotherapy has borrowed some of its best tools from religion: confession, assurance, guidance, acceptance. The pastoral counselor who has learned much from psychotherapy can deal with problems of normal guilt, which is his special province, with new assurance. As Tillich has said: "Psychotherapy can liberate one from a special difficulty. Religion shows to him who is liberated, and has to decide about the meaning and aim of his existence, a final way. This difference is decisive for the independence as well as for the co-operation of religion and psychotherapy."

What I have implied in this chapter is what I style the eleventh commandment: "Thou shalt grow." Certainly the best of psychiatric and religious insight will agree that growth is the goal of life. Freud in his researches proved that life is purposive, that there is *meaning* in all our actions from the smallest to the greatest, for they are related to our deepest needs and desires. Sartre, the existentialist, finds life meaningless and absurd, but he must deal with the existential fact that many people find life meaningful and significant. The anxious child needs a great deal of love and assurance in order to grow and ultimately find meaning for his life, but all human beings in order to grow need love, which has been styled "the supreme form of energy."

7

THE RESPONSIBLE SELF

ON A CHILLY GRAY DAY in the early years of World War II a young man stood in a line of shivering prisoners. "What's that under your coat?" snarled a sadistic guard. "Just some paper, sir." "What kind of paper?" "Oh, the manuscript of a book I m writing." "Ah," said the guard. "I like books. Let me see it." The unsuspecting author handed over the manuscript, and then with one sweep of his arm, the guard took it and flung it into a fire he had lighted to warm himself against the November chill.

The young author despairingly watched the result of years of study and work turn to ashes and smoke. He then shuffled down the line into the living death of Auschwitz, one of Adolf Hitler's concentration camps. The day before, he had been a professional man, a respected doctor, and hospital director. Now divested of everything that makes for dignity and honor and the significance of a human being, he fell into deep despair. These condemned men were stripped of their clothing and all personal possessions: watches, pens, glasses, money, identification. The prisoners were even shaved of all body hair. They were allowed to keep dentures, but these would be removed, along with gold inlays if any, after their death in a gas chamber. A number was tattooed on the arm, and each was given the rags of a wretched prisoner who had been cremated the previous week.

Ahead of him lay further physical degradation, emotional scarification, and the kind of mental and spiritual suffering of

the men upon whom were heaped unbelievable indignities an
extraordinary cruelties. The poet Wordsworth during th
French Revolution was appalled by its excesses and wrote mo
ingly about the inhumanity of man to man. But what Word
worth saw in the French Revolution was as boys playing co
and robbers compared to what men endured in the Nazi co
centration and extermination camps. I myself as a young gra
uate student saw the high fence being constructed around wh
was to become the infamous concentration camp at Dacha
Twenty years later, again studying, this time in Vienna, drivi
by Dachau, I could not bear to enter with the casual curiosit
of a tourist. Too many ghosts peopled those sad premises, an
I was sickened at the thought of what happened there. Whe
I shared these feelings recently with a friend, who is a Jewis
rabbi, he said to me, "You should not avoid such experiences.
I had also told him I hated to see movies or read books abo
the Nazi era in Germany, and I asked him why he replied s
to me. "Because it was not all evil. Poignant poetry and son
came out of the camps." And again I found myself thinkin
of those early student days in Marburg, Germany. The Naz
had launched a particularly violent campaign of vilification
the Jews. Every Jewish store in town was picketed by stalwa
blackshirted elite guards of Hitler, the hated S.S. Shoulderin
my way past them, I walked into the store owned by a Jewis
friend. Going up to him, I gave him very unchristian comfor
"Wouldn't you like to shoot those thugs outside your store?"
cried angrily. Putting his arm around my shoulder, he sai
"Friend, Israel is exceedingly old and has seen this persecutic
before. Long after Hitler's bones have turned to dust Isra
will still be here." How true his words have turned out to b
despite Hitler's effort to exterminate the Jewish people with a
order that murdered six million of them.

Let us return to the prisoner in Auschwitz of whom I spok
earlier. Thrusting his hands into the pockets of his ragge
clothes, he felt a scrap of paper. Pulling it out, the young ma
found a page from the Jewish prayerbook, and on it was printe

the Shema Yisrael: "Hear, O Israel: The Lord our God is one Lord; and you shall love the Lord your God with all your heart, and with all your soul, and with all your might." Later the prisoner was able to say, thinking of his burned manuscript, "I took this as a sign that henceforth I was to *live* my thoughts instead of merely writing them down." He also was to learn what many had learned before him: truth, whether religious doctrine, philosophic wisdom, or scientific principle, is always experienced before it is verbalized. This may sound abstract, but real truth comes from encounter and is abstracted from experience. Moses' unmistakable experience of God in the deserts of Egypt enabled him to speak authoritatively concerning the character of God. Martin Luther's struggles and his experience of complete acceptance by God had to precede his formal statement of the great principles of the Protestant Reformation. And when Viktor Frankl, of whom I am writing, states that man has a freedom and a unique capacity to transcend—rise above— the strangling and often remorseless forces of heredity and environment, he speaks with authority. For Frankl speaks out of the experience of the deadly environment of the concentration camp and of a heredity, his Jewishness, that placed him there.

Who is this man, and what does he have to say to us, who are not prisoners, but who nevertheless feel the limitations of heredity and often complain that we are controlled by environment which may be represented by taxes, an unhappy home, a confining job, serious illness, or "those guys in Washington"? Viktor Frankl is a doctor, a psychiatrist and a neurologist, whose home is Vienna, Austria. Those of us who have visited there know the the beauty and charm of the place even after two world wars destroyed much of its wealth and empire. Vienna is the home of many modern methods of psychotherapy. It was the home of Freud, father of psychoanalysis, of Moreno, father of group therapy, of Adler, father of your inferiority complexes. Beethoven spent many years there, and it was the home of Martin Buber, famous philosopher and theologian.

Carrying on this tradition, Frankl helped establish some of

the first Youth Guidance Centers in Vienna. At the outbreak of the war he headed the same mental hospital that Moreno had previously supervised. When the Nazi government decided that certain patients were incurable and were to be sent to the gas chamber, Frankl changed their diagnoses to more benign diseases, and saved their lives for perhaps a few more weeks. Ultimately came the concentration camp, for, according to Nazi race theory, the Jews were subhuman. In the camps men with brilliant minds—scientists, doctors, lawyers, businessmen, skilled workers—lived under the rudest of conditions on a diet close to starvation. They performed hard labor on roads and factories with hand tools that often were broken. If a man faltered at work or became gray from fatigue or illness, his number might be chosen for the next quota for the gas chamber. For inspections, men would scrape their whiskers with broken glass, having no razors of course. This would impart a false ruddiness to their cheeks. When they were transferred to a new camp, a guard would indicate with a nod to right or left lines whether a man was good for a few more days' work or was to be sent immediately to the gas chamber.

Under such appalling conditions men discussed the whole matter of life and death in the darkness of the barracks after lights went out at night. What is human existence? What is its meaning? Can a life of such meaningless suffering have any significance or purpose? With their own existence at stake, men discussed the existence of God. Is there a God? If so, why a concentration camp, its sadistic inhumanity of man to man? If there is no God, does life end in nothingness? Or is there a God, but one who is too weak for our needs? These questions were not new; they just arrived in a new environment. They have always been asked by the existentialists from Pascal and Kierkegaard to Nietzsche and Sartre. These questions are as old as thinking man. Kierkegaard said that our churches imprison God. Nietzsche said that our churches are the tomb of God. Sartre says that "God is nonexistent. We must shoulder the responsibilities we formerly laid upon God."

There was an easy answer to the questions: "To go against the wire"—the electrified wire. Suicide was an easy way out, but no real solution. Frankl argued desperately against this with the intensity of the physician who takes his Oath of Hippocrates most seriously. It is one thing to answer philosophical questions around the dinner table or in the classroom. It is another matter to face them existentially, in the day-to-day existence of a concentration camp, where theory came slam-bang up against hard facts. Frankl already had worked through his own despair at losing his book manuscript. He writes:

I realized that a life whose meaning depended upon publishing a manuscript would not be worth living.

What was really needed was a fundamental change in our attitude toward life. We had to learn ourselves, and furthermore to teach despairing men, that it really did not matter what we expected from life, but rather what life expected from us. We needed to stop asking about the meaning of life, and instead to think of ourselves as being those who were being questioned by life daily and hourly. Life ultimately means taking the responsibility to find the right answer to its Problems, and to fulfill the tasks which it constantly sets before each individual.

These tasks and therefore the purpose and values in life differ from man to man, and from moment to moment. Thus it is impossible to define the purpose of life in a general way. "Life" does not mean something vague, but something very real and concrete, just as life's tasks are very real and concrete. They form man's destiny, which is different and unique for each individual. No situation repeats itself and each situation calls for a different response. Sometimes the situation in which a man finds himself may require him to shape his own destiny by action. Sometimes a man may be required simply to accept fate, to bear his cross.

When a man finds that it is his destiny to suffer, he will have to accept suffering as his task; his single and unique task. He will have to struggle for the realization that even in suffering he is unique and alone in the universe. No man can relieve him of his suffering, or suffer in his place. His unique opportunity lies in the way in which he bears his burden.

Gordon Allport, writing the introduction to Frankl's book on the death camps, says:

Here we encounter a central theme of existentialism: To live is to suffer—to survive is to find meaning in the suffering. If there is any purpose in life at all, there must be purpose in suffering and in dying. But no man can tell another what this purpose is. Each must find out for himself, and must accept the responsibility that his answer prescribes. If he succeeds, he will continue to GROW in spite of all indignities. Frankl is fond of quoting Nietzsche, "He who has a WHY to live can bear with almost any HOW."

In the concentration camps practically every circumstance conspired to make the prisoner lose his hold. All the familiar goals in life were snatched away. What remained was the last of human freedoms, and maybe one of the most significant: the ability to choose one's attitude in a given set of circumstances. This ultimate freedom, recognized by ancient Stoics as well as by modern existentialists, took on vivid significance in Frankl's story. The prisoners on the whole were only average men, but some, at least, by choosing to be worthy of their suffering, proved man's capacity to rise above his outward fate.

It must be noted here that the concentration camp was a tragic laboratory of intense living, that is, an enlargement or magnification of problems we all face in life: the tensions of business; the unhappy disagreements as to policy and goal; the problems of working under an unfair foreman, or a superior officer, or executive, who vents his spleen on subordinates; the unhappy problems that almost everyone goes out to face on a Monday morning. The list could be extended to include the clash of interests and demands of the job, parent-child relations, difficulties of adolescence in its search for identity, marital problems, racial conflicts, political upheavals, and the impending sense of uncertainty and doom that overshadows so many lives in the twentieth century.

The kind of suffering and the dilemma of decision confronting the concentration camp prisoners was vividly depicted by Shakespeare in the soliloquy of Hamlet:

> To be, or not to be: that is the question.
> Whether 't is nobler in the mind to suffer
> The slings and arrows of outrageous fortune,
> Or to take arms against a sea of troubles,
> And by opposing end them. To die; to sleep;
> No more; and by a sleep to say we end
> The heart-ache and the thousand natural shocks
> That flesh is heir to. 'T is a consummation
> Devoutly to be wish'd. To die; to sleep;—

To the question, "To be, or not to be?" Viktor Frankl answers with a great affirmation: Man's being is also such that he is to be different from every other form of being. He is unique. There is absolutely no other being exactly like him. Because of his difference, his uniqueness, he is responsible therefore for the fullest possible development of his own capacities, gifts, and powers of self-expression. Human existence carries with it the power of transcendence, the power than man has to rise above himself, above his predicaments, and the power of changing or transmuting those predicaments into achievements. I return again to the conversation with my friend, the Jewish rabbi, cited earlier. He had chided me for my negative reaction to books and movies of the Hitler era. "In the concentration camps," he said, "there was a saying: 'One of us must live, one of us at least must survive.'" To my question, "Why just one?" he replied, "One—to tell the story!" It matters not that more than one survived "to tell the story." After all, eyewitnesses, photographs, and criminal trials have served to tell the whole gruesome story. But this is to miss the point the rabbi insisted upon. The very determination that at least "one must survive" put the responsibility for survival upon each man, giving each man a *raison d'être*, "a reason for being," for staying alive as long as possible, in order that the lamentable story might be told. This responsibility in turn enabled men to rise above and to bear with the rigors of prison camp life for the sake of a more important goal that was beyond the self and its present suffering.

The responsible self is characterized by his transcendence, his ability to stand outside the very real forces that limit life and action. Such forces can be and often are very strong and even frightening, but stronger still in the man who maintains his ability to stand off, to analyze and judge them, and make his decision as to how to meet them. I have chosen to tell the story of Frankl's concentration camp experiences at some length because in a very definite way it is an extended illustration of most of the emphases in this book. I have mentioned transcendence in several contexts and it remains an illuminating philosophical concept. In the concentration camp, however, it was so much more than a bit of philosophy, a helpful idea. It became a way of life with deeper implications than mere survival value, for it enabled a man to see beyond himself. Those who could not do this were condemned by their own frustration to either apathy or a bitter, hopeless defiance. In the camps certain prisoners were temporarily made overseers, though they knew they too were destined ultimately for the gas chamber. Unable to transcend their fate, they worked out their bitter frustrations on their fellow prisoners and as a result were more feared and hated than were the Nazi guards. Apathy caused by what appeared to be absolutely meaningless suffering brought many men to an early death. This result was also observed among Americans in the prison camps of the Korean war. Many young men overcome by their feeling of the hopelessness of their condition sank into apathy, withdrew from all communication with others, and died. Doctors could find no other cause for their death than that they had lost their will to live, to keep going.

Jean-Paul Sartre is well known as a philosopher of existentialism. Viktor Frankl has developed a type of psychotherapy called existential analysis. It is also called logotherapy because it is directed toward the achievement of meaning (Greek, *logos*) in one's personal life. Of all the writers who deal with human existence and with the philosophy and psychology of existentialism none have a better right to the field than Sartre and Frankl. Sartre fought throughout World War II in the French underground and his experiences there made some mystery novels appear tame by comparison. His writings are colored by the facts of his own existence, often a very precarious existence during the Occupation of France. His conclusions about human existence are pessimistic. His gripping play *No Exit* seems to decide that "Hell is—other people." Agreeing with Nietzsche that God is dead, he makes a most theological affirmation when he urges that man must now assume responsibility for the burdens he formerly laid on God's shoulders. I am sure that when he first said that a Homeric shout of joy was heard in heaven. This is what the theologians have been trying to teach for centuries: ethical responsibility. No more the childish, "Let George (God) do it," but: Grow up to the full stature of manhood and grapple with the forces that would determine your life and shoulder the responsibilities that are yours!

Frankl's conclusions about human nature, sharply honed under war conditions even more appalling than those Sartre faced, are diametrically opposite to the views of Sartre. He is optimistic and has a profound Jewish experience of the reality of God. Both men, in spite of widely varying viewpoints, give a high place to the role of responsibility in human existence. In his psychiatric practice Frankl often uses the call to responsibility as an effective therapeutic tool. I have seen him do this most emphatically in clinical demonstrations before a large class of medical students. A man who had attempted suicide because of having been discharged from his position was interviewed in a very considerate, kindly manner to get at the causes of his difficulty. When it developed that the man had an invalid wife, confined to a wheelchair, a wife whom he protested he deeply loved, Frankl's manner changed abruptly. He did not actually commit "verbal assault and battery" upon the patient, but sternly admonished him as to his responsibility to his wife. The clinic might help him get another job, but as to his wife—who would love her and care for her if he died a suicide? In effect, he was told to get out of the narrow circle of self-concern and think of something bigger than self—his responsibility to others. The patient, who had been visibly depressed and apathetic up to this point, braced his shoulders, looked up with a smile, and said, "You've got something there."

Readers who are astonished at this type of "therapeutic inter-vention" might well read Standal and Corsini's *Critical Inci-dents in Psychotherapy,* where similar procedures with gratifying results are reported. The plain truth is that the human being, for all his capacities, shrinks back from responsibility and the tasks that it represents. In part, our shrinking is the result of a carry-over of nineteenth-century determinism that still seeps into modern education. Heisenberg and other physicists have conclusively proved that atoms do not always "obey" certain "natural laws." This has blown the old deterministic views of cause and effect sky-high, but the faith in determinism lingers on. A concomitant factor is the influence of Freudian psychol-ogy, which, though waning, still is influential among many people who but recently have become acquainted with it, thanks to the prolificacy of paperback reprints. Freud's psychology was deterministic and pessimistic, it is true: but, as stated elsewhere, Freud's lifetime devotion to the task of circumventing the re-sults of previously determined conditions shows the happy in-consistency of all great men. The id (German, *es,* "it"), the unconscious storehouse of all experiences, can and does exert tremendous, "irrational" influence in our lives. But man is still man, his rational nature sets him above the beasts and above nature. He *can* perceive his negative self—his outrigger; he *can* transcend very real limits of heredity and environment. This is because he is more than an irrational unconscious id, he is an ego which is rational, conscious, able to choose, to decide. In his later years Freud gave more importance to the ego, and an emphasis on ego-psychology was the result.

The person who is aware of his capacity to transcend himself, to detach himself from self and from the world, can encounter himself, or even oppose himself when necessary. This was dis-cussed when I treated dividedness, but to amplify the thought here: the person who transcends his dividedness is genuinely able to assume responsibility for his actions. He now sees that there are no real excuses outside himself and can make his de-cisions accordingly. He is up above looking down on the self wriggling around trying to find excuses. "This is because my father was cruel to me"; or, "It's what everybody does"; and the defeated, "That's the way things are." To the delinquent child who glibly defends himself with, "I came from a broken home," Dr. Glasser replies, "You are in Juvenile Hall because you stole a car, that is the reality factor." An unhappy platitude has it that a child of divorced parents is doomed to marital unhappiness. This is a logical conclusion of an application of deterministic theory to human existence, overlooking the fact that humans are unique. Contradicting the platitude is the fact that several people of my acquaintance are from broken homes. They have made exceptionally happy marriages precisely because they themselves determined not to let the failures of parents be the dominant factors in their own lives.

A corollary to the fact of human transcendence is the affirmation of man's freedom. It cannot be denied that a great many things in our lives are determining factors. "Can a man by thinking add one inch to his height?" Adler may not have been influenced by the Biblical question, but he built an imposing psychological structure on the idea and fact of organ inferiority. It *is* hard for a five-foot man to compete in a world of six footers. But he is still free to decide whether to solve the dilemma with bitter, aggressive craftiness, or to develop his mental and emotional capacities, so that he becomes a giant of the intellect. A tragic element in the race tension of America is precisely the results of certain predetermined conditions. Most white men cannot think and feel themselves into the mental and emotional life of a man born black. The sharecropper may lead a more miserable existence than many blacks, but his desperate ego is strengthened by a most flimsy prop: his feeling of superiority over the black. Though the white may never feel black, because determined by heredity, parents, traditions, culture, he is capable of *thinking* black to the point of transcending blind prejudice and aiding in decisions that result in more justice and equal opportunity for *blacks*. The concerned white uses his freedom in action designed to overcome some glaring defects in our culture which were "determined" by the sins of our ancestral slave traders.

Existentialists of all kinds assert the existence of man's freedom. That man remains free under any or all circumstances
seems to be a very bold type of whistling in the dark. Where is
freedom in a prison, in a hospital bed with an incurable disease,
in a concentration camp fenced with electrified barbed wire?
The answer to this often despairing and sometimes cynical
question can be found in the nature of freedom as a precious pos-
session of the responsible self. The range of such freedom may
be quite small, but its significance is not diminished by the
relativity of range. I think of carbon, which is found in a concentrated form in anthracite coal, sometimes so clean that it
scarcely soils the hands. A still purer form of carbon is found
in the diamond that most people prefer over coal or over the
carborundum jewelry grandmother wore before she learned that
it was produced by the ton. Freedom to make choices may be
exceedingly small, but it remains genuine. The brilliance of a
quarter-carat diamond is not affected by its size. This is what
men discovered in concentration camps: their freedom to choose
the attitude of despair or of integrity with which to face inevitable suffering. "To live is to suffer" is a theme we may not
like, but it is one the writers on human existence will not let us
forget. Our television culture may make men increasingly cal-
lous to suffering, as were the crowds in the Roman stadium.
After all, television is primarily entertainment and distraction,
is it not? Even though life may spare him personal and physical suffering, no sensitive person can watch terrified civilians
fleeing a napalm bombing in Vietnam, or see heads split with
stout hickory clubs in a street demonstration, without suffering
and remorse for "man's inhumanity to man."

Man's ability to transcend himself and his culture is tested
by his use of the freedom that activates or throws his transcendence into high gear, so that he moves out of frustration and
apathy into action. Freedom is a gift that, like time itself, must
be used responsibly. Frankl teaches that responsibility is an
exceedingly personal and individual matter. It is never a vague
generalization but is definite and specific. A man is always
responsible *to* someone—to family, society, morality, duty, na-

tion or God. The exuberance of liberation from enslaving forces needs to be tempered by the responsible use of that freedom. Otherwise freedom rapidly transposes into that license of the childish "I want what I want when I want it" variety. Progressive educational institutions that dare to allow students the freedom to participate in policy-making decisions of the schools are learning that students can exercise their new freedom in a most responsible way. The current agitation to give youth the full rights of citizenship at the age of eighteen is in recognition of this fact that they can be trusted with responsibility, even as they are depended upon to defend their country at that age.

Dr. Richard Cabot, a pioneer in urging the rapprochement of religion and therapy, wrote a best seller entitled *What Men Live By* (1914). Though not always consciously aware of it, we live by or according to the values that are most important to us. The values that Cabot thought pre-eminent are work, play, love, and worship. When Freud was asked the question of values he reduced Cabot's selection to *Lieben und Arbeiten,* "love and work." In Frankl's thought, values are not listed specifically but are treated under three categories—experiential, creative, and attitudinal. Experiential values are realized when one is sensitive and receptive to beauty and truth in nature, in art, and in life itself. A desert sunset, the thunder of breakers on a reef, a Beethoven symphony, the consolation of an understanding friend—these are but a few of the many experiences that add value to living. Creative values are related to acts and accomplishments that utilize at least some of the unique capacities that every human being possesses. Creativity is not limited to artist and poet, for everyone has his own gifts to give, his own tasks to fulfill. One's creative capacities that have been suppressed, unused because of inertia or sheer laziness or denied expression for various other reasons can result in neurosis. When this happens the victim may seek psychotherapy to alleviate his neurotic distress, frustration, and existential boredom. The therapist with insight moves quickly into vocational guidance and works with his client in terms of the practicable ways of activating his dormant creativity. It is my feeling that far too much of what is called vocational guidance is oriented merely to work, to the job, and to the size of the paycheck. I have known many successful men who gave up lucrative positions precisely because they were lucrative—and only that! Their sense of vocation was not fulfilled in the work they had, and they craved a deeper dimension of meaning in their lives, one that did not necessarily have to be found apart from the daily tasks. Such men are aware of Frankl's idea of vocation. Because every man is unique, he has a mission, a call, a specific task that he alone can carry out.

Where a life has been constricted in experimental and creative values it still can achieve greatness in its attitudes. The way in which one faces whatever life has to offer, its successes and failures, its rewards and its painful punishments, its health and its sickness, its glory and its guilt, this is the way to attitudinal value. You cannot learn this from books or lectures. A value system can be codified and memorized, but it does not become a part of a personal life until it is lived. You can learn *about* love from books and from people. But you do not know love until you yourself are loving, and in loving you become lovable. Values are like that, for they become real, a part of you only when you live them. Your attitude toward life, whether it is meaningful or meaningless, has a tremendous impact on your decisions with regard to the problems, isolation, conflicts, and "dividedness" that are shared by all!

Suffering and death often, but not always, seem so meaningless to the sufferer and to the dying, who have every right to the question, "Why?" Our whole culture is definitely at fault here, for we falter at the task of teaching men how to live and we ignore the necessity of facing inevitable death even as we shrink back from suffering. Plato's poignant account of the last hours of Socrates shows how a responsible self calmly, even serenely, faced approaching death, not forgetting, and admonishing a companion to pay a small debt that he owed to a friend. Tolstoy's account of *The Death of Ivan Ilych* is a vivid contrast to the death of Socrates, as Ivan screamed in his futile fright in order to ward off the approaching specter. Yet in the last hours of his life he found meaning in his hitherto meaningless life, and the darkness of death was transmuted into brilliant light. Many suffering people conquer their illnesses by their attitude toward them long before disease triumphs over their bodies. A friend, victim of incurable and inoperable cancer, which requires frequent and painful treatments, speaks of it as casually as a person reporting that he has a toothache. As an avocation he plays clarinet in a Dixieland band and is its most radiant member. When he is absent for hospitalization, the band, in the words of Willie Loman's son (in Miller's *Death of a Salesman*), "can't get with it." If a very sick man can vitalize a dance band, what does this say to people who are relatively healthy? I am reminded of the story of the student, paralyzed by polio from the waist down, who reported on his summer spent in a state hospital for retarded children. When asked by a fellow student how he as an exceptionally intelligent man could relate to retarded people, he replied simply, "Well, you see, I'm in a wheelchair." "Ah, yes," his questioner returned, "you have an advantage over us there." Most of us would not like to have "the advantage" of a wheelchair, but we can see that this man's attitudinal values carried him far in relating to his fellowman and for their benefit as well as for his own. If significance and meaning can be found in disability, suffering, and in death itself, it follows that all life has meaning. The search for meaning is the task of every individual to carry on in his own particular way. This viewpoint could add a new dimension to the popular distress over the way of the "hippies."

Man is ultimately faced with the choice of two decisions: that life is absurd (with Camus), or that life is meaningful (with Frankl). That life is fraught with meaning is the conviction that can be a powerful weapon in the armamentarium of psychotherapy. The therapist does not prescribe meaning as the doctor prescribes aspirin for headache; he helps the client find the meaning that is uniquely his. If a patient asks Frankl, "What is the meaning of life for me," he is likely to get a Socratic answer: "What is the best chess move?" Most powerful of all the human drives, Frankl thinks, is man's will to meaning.

When this is not met or frustrated he falls ill or his life is warped or stunted. Meaning is most often discovered in that which is beyond the self and greater than the self. The responsible self has learned with Scheler that "only he who loses himself in a worthy cause can gain a genuine self."

8

THE COMPLETE SELF

THE COMPLETE SELF has a great secret that colors and energizes his total life. The secret is not unlike that of Tournier's child who begins his deeper socialization when he tells his friend instead of his mommy. The child has taken a significant step from the security of the past, where his mother was the confidant, to the uncertainty of the future by his own decision to confide in his friend of the present. The secret of the complete self is that he has learned to live in the present, in present time. Today's frequent lament of being rushed for time, in a hurry, time-minded, and the mourning of the speedy passage of time do not dominate him. He is not time-bound. He has learned the secret of holding in check, of properly evaluating, of successfully surmounting, the demonic forces that rob us of time. When we are deprived of time we are robbed of our very life, swindled in the arena of living, for the present is all the time that we have. The past is already gone, the future not yet here! Theodor Bovet, the Swiss psychiatrist, calls time the essence of life, but "time also is not an inexorable, austere, pacemaker governed by the swing of a clock pendulum, hurrying us through our life, demolishing our previous work, and finally conducting us to our death. It is much more our framework, according to which we unfold and realize ourselves, and which finally guides us to another aspect and another time."

The complete self knows that time is the essence of life. He is like a sturdy tree "planted by streams of water, that yields its fruit in its season, and its leaf does not wither, in all that he does, he prospers!" The well-rooted tree draws nourishment from the earth even as its branches and leaves draw life-giving energy from the sun. Because the complete self is like a tree (to him the earth and the sun are past and future), he finds it difficult to comprehend what the philosophers mean when they speak of "man's alienation from nature." His experience and understanding of nature is similar to that of Eric Jaensch's eidetic type who is in "loving coherence with Nature," with its life and beauty.

Alienation from himself is not his problem either. He quickly recognizes the temptation to play the phony and so he is his honest self most of the time. When he does not disclose himself he is quite aware that he is playing a role. As a consequence his genuiness is often a source of embarrassment to his friends and others who are habituated to false fronts, masks, and duplicity —the practice of hiding one's true feelings and attitudes for lack of trust in others. He has his share of conflicts but has learned to engage himself and exercise the muscles of decision. He is aware of the dangers of the isolated self but he values the opportunity to be alone, because he is not running away from himself. He has recognized and appropriated his dividedness so that it works for him and his goals and he does not tear himself apart. He therefore has time, time to live life to its fullest possibilities in each ongoing moment of the present. Past mistakes, sins, yesterday's opportunities lost, failure in the past, do not crowd into his responsible work of today. Nor do worries, forebodings, and anxieties for future possibilities keep him from today's necessary decisions. He is characterized by the capacity for independence qualified by a reasonable dependence on others, for he has learned with John Donne that "no man is an island." His days are filled with adequate time—time to carry out the tasks and responsibilities of each day. He is not alienated from nature, from himself, or from his fellowman.

A great many people do not present the picture of the complete person. The days of their years pass all too quickly and they never have time to really live. They echo the words of the psalmist: "My days pass away like smoke." Projects are started but never completed—for lack of time. Important decisions are postponed or all too hurriedly made because of the pressure of time. The importunate student approaches the important professor with his hesitant request: "I know you are so busy, sir, but could you . . . ?" Both are rushed for time. But why? And what is the reason for the existence of the professor if not for the needs of the student? The harassed professor has adequate time for "research," but not for living, for encountering the live student. An hour's time invested in the student might change the course of a man's life—and this has happened frequently enough. It might even change the teacher's life, give him an idea he could get in no other way. On the other hand, another research paper might gain the teacher a promotion! Time! It is so precious. How to spend it, how to utilize it to the best advantage, is not so much the question as is the lament that there is not enough of it available. Theodor Bovet, in his book *Have Time and Be Free,* adds up meticulously the appointments, preparations for lectures, and other duties of his average ten-hour working day. The total sum, however, adds up to thirteen hours. All of us face this dilemma, and in attempting to solve it we grasp at the compromise of urgency and hurry.

The swift passage of time tempts some to brood upon the futility of life. In their world view and the place of self in it they tend to agree with the somber words of the psalmist: "As for man, his days are like grass; he flourishes like the flower of the field; for the wind passes over it, and it is gone, and its place knows it no more." Sartre and other existentialists have nowhere stated this view more succinctly. In their absorption with the past they mournfully agree with Shakespeare, who in *Henry VIII,* states: "Men's evil manners live in brass; their virtues We write in water." The story is told of Oliver Edwards, who accosted Samuel Johnson on the street one day with the remark: "I have tried too in my time to be a philosopher; but I don't know how, cheerfulness was always breaking in." Johnson was a sturdy oak of a man, but his friend was far more than mere grass. He had learned that whereas grass is much the same everywhere, nature does produce a great variety of trees. His life may have been like that of the graceful willow, bending before the storm but not breaking, while the oak has strength to defy the force of the wind. It takes time to produce a tree, and the tree has time to grow and "yield its fruit in its season." The direction of its growth is vertical rather than horizontal like creeping bent grass.

Grass people are time-bound and time-limited. They take the linear view of life, peering anxiously at the coming of evening when "the wind passes over" and the grass "fades and withers." Since they are concerned with the future, their present time is progressively foreshortened by the exact amount of time spent in anxiety for what might be coming next. They never become complete selves; often they dare not even get onto the highway toward completion, preferring a safe country lane of childhood that really goes nowhere. Their energies, as Erich Fromm delineates in *Man for Himself*, never are successfully integrated, focused on meaningful projects. Lacking integration, such energies then become canalized into lopsided emphases. Prejudice and fanaticism seem normal; fear and anxiety dominate; and hostility is arranged against the vague "they" who always are seeking to run and ruin one's life.

The complete self is one who has learned to handle the past and to evaluate the future properly. Correspondingly, his present time is adequate for the challenges, work, and decisions of the day. The self often can become a cage in which man is imprisoned. The caged self peers out through very real, if invisible, strong bars. When well "institutionalized" or a successful "organization man," he does not even want to leave the cage. In extreme cases he is not even aware of his imprisonment, for a sad acquiescence has become normative. This is not without its lighter moments. When I was working on the staff of a state mental hospital I became well acquainted with an elderly but yet vivacious patient. She had been in the hospital so long that it was her only real home and she enjoyed the simple housekeeping tasks assigned to her. Born in Germany, she delighted in my efforts to converse with her in her native tongue. One day she greeted me with: "Doctor, don't you wish you were crazy like us? We can sing, dance, and play when we feel like it, but you have to be sober, serious, and hard-working." She no longer knew or missed freedom. I had to return to another way of life at the end of the day.

The invisible bars enclosing the caged self are the powerful unconscious forces within stemming from past experience, and these often conflict with duties, demands, and desires of today. Unconscious memories, unhappy experiences of the past, neurotic and very real guilt can bind us more effectively than the stoutest of cords. Psychoanalysis has successfully led many people from the cage by patient dredging up of all the repressed unhappy shadowy material of the unconscious. However, the chains that bind us to the unconscious, though very real, often have rusty links not impossible to break. Therapists like Rogers, Perls, Ellis, Lazarus, and many more, also seem successful in freeing caged victims. Their methods have many names. Existential therapy, Gestalt therapy, behavior therapy, rational-emotive therapy are but a few. All have in common the tendency largely to ignore the past with its unconscious material and to begin where the patient is today, with today's problems and issues. Increasingly in their efforts to motivate and guide their clients, therapists are becoming sensitive to future time and the hope it presents.

A most positive element in the dividedness of man is our two-fold need to be alone and also to be in community. The "courage to be" oneself requires both. The self can become a very lonely cage if it remains the sole citadel of life, the only place one can feel safe and secure. The self by itself is not adequate for security, and the man who peers out from his inner retreat is aptly described by today's familiar words: isolation, loneliness, alienation, meaninglessness. The behavioral and personality sciences may never come to agreement or any unification of their findings, but this important truth from their research stands out like a mountain peak: Self-development demands aloneness, the ability to be alone, to meditate, to plan, even to pray! The great state universities now offer courses on how to meditate. The companion truth of man's dividedness is that his self-actualization also demands community: communal action and involvement. This action is more than just being cozy in a clique (even some therapy groups are marked by clique appeal!), or demonstrating in a highly excited crowd. Such ways of reacting come about when we emulate the herd or regress to the point where some atavistic herd instinct drives us, effectively short-circuiting our intelligence. Animals huddle in herds for protection. They stampede in herds when confused and fearful. Man in contrast has created community, a distinct improvement over the herd. Community, then, offers the only viable escape from the confining cage of the self. One who cannot enter into community is condemned to a lonely half-existence, a modern Robinson Crusoe without his man Friday, alone on an island washed by seas of humanity that he dare not venture out upon. He is afraid to swim, and he denies his canoe its necessary outrigger.

Community that is "for real" is shot through with concern and commitment, the two most important colors in the spectrum of love. One who does not know love and who therefore cannot love had better beware of community. Philip Rieff correctly calls love "the supreme form of energy." Such energy is like high-voltage electricity. Nobody denies or affronts its power with impunity. One cannot come to community with a two-volt battery of self-love and find what he seeks. Phony or not, he will be taken as one. All the commitment and concern that he has is directed internally, upon self, and he has not the necessary voltage to work within community.

Social action is directed toward community, and it used to be a small force of intelligent men of concern needling the membership of the more progressive churches to get involved in the world. Today social action is on the streets, on the campus, in the struggle for civil and human rights, and it is still trying to break into the churches. Despite excesses and manipulatory movements of some chauvinistic, fanatical leaders, no one acquainted with the idealism of modern youth can deny the genuine energy, the high voltage of their concern and love. Of course many adults are shocked by the voltage. They bandage the wound with prejudice, resort to stereotypes and name-calling, and retreat behind the safe, high walls of the inner self where things are always as they used to be. They have forgotten James Russell Lowell: "New occasions teach new duties, Time makes ancient good uncouth." More seriously, they have forgotten the prophet's warning: "Woe to you who lay field to field and deprive the widow and orphan of their inheritance." But our concerned youth have not forgotten, and their action uncomfortably reminds us of the widows and orphans created by the American policy in Vietnam. There is more prophetic judgment of our ways, our culture, our institutions in our youth than this world dreams of. This has not come about through mischievousness but through concern and energetic love. The "generation gap" is one more illustration of dividedness, into young and old, but can we stop criticizing long enough to listen, to learn?

One of Hitler's last victims, executed a few days before Hitler's suicide, was Dietrich Bonhoeffer. His whole life was one of concern and commitment, and his writings cut sharply across the twofold necessity of aloneness and community that I have been discussing. He maintains that many people move toward community because they are afraid to be alone. "Let him who cannot be alone beware of community. Let him who is not in community beware of being alone." The dynamics of self-actualization and community involvement can scarcely be spelled out any more clearly. In his book *Life Together,* Bonhoeffer continues: "The person who comes into a fellowship because he is running away from himself is misusing it for the sake of diversion—no matter how spiritual this diversion may appear. He is not really seeking community at all, but only the distraction which will allow him to forget his loneliness for a brief time—the very alienation that creates the deadly isolation of man."

Coming out of the civil rights movement are specific examples that highlight Bonhoeffer's judgment. Among my friends are many people who were and still are involved in the civil rights movement. These include workers in SCLC, SNCC,

Quaker groups, and also the Peace Corps. Some have worked for a three-month summer period, others for three years of volunteer or subsistence pay work. These young persons report that people who entered the program to solve their own personal problems were usually so conflicted that they had to be asked to resign. The negative side of their dividedness, which they were unable to incorporate, created more difficulties that in turn were detrimental to the cause they were seeking to serve. Such people, however, represent only a small minority of the workers. One young woman after three years of such service returned to college with a firm goal: to earn a degree in social science so that she could return better trained for the work that she now realized was the vocation of her life. At the early age of twenty she had experienced the values of aloneness and had effectively participated in community. Though she was hurrying to a late-afternoon psychology class as we talked, she remarked, "I am glad that I now have time for the important things I want to do." Her words serve to sharpen the theme with which I began this chapter: time and the complete self.

It is my contention that many people, indeed most of the people we are acquainted with, do not have time to live, and of course they do not have time for love! I mean this literally. There is little time—actual, 24-hours-a-day time, clock time—for us to live and to love. This is because influences, memories, forces, habits from the past—Tillich would call them demonic—rush in and demand our consideration, and this consumes precious time of the present. Too often we are tied to the past by our guilt for what has happened in the past. We cannot accept ourselves because of what has occurred, our weakness, failure, sins of yesteryear. These haunt us, ride us, drive in relentlessly and continuously from the past into the present. We are like the character in Bunyan's *The Pilgrim's Progress* with the burden on his back. Our problem is that we similarly carry a large sack on our backs into which we stuff each day's sorry failures, sins, missed opportunities. Unable to accept ourselves as we are—divided, problematic, conflicted—we also are unable to see that others—family, friends, and God—accept us in spite of our being unacceptable. Even when the past dominates a man to the extent that he gives up, lives completely in the past, and becomes ill, psychotic, his family and friends often continue to accept him. Their acceptance and concern are some of the best sources of healing. Every psychotherapist is aware of the factor of time as it involves the psychotically ill person. If his problem revolves around guilt for whatever happened in the past, that is where he actually lives from day to day. He literally is not in the present. He has no "today," for his time is spent with remorse or justification of yesterday. Guilt, conscious and unconscious, real and neurotic guilt orders his day and consumes the time thereof. Thus he carries the past with him wherever he goes and the past with its guilt, regret, remorse, avidly eats away at the present.

A similar phenomenon affects people who have not come to terms with future time. The man who lives in the past is emasculated by guilt. The person who lives with foreboding for the future is enervated by anxiety. His anxiety drives him to the frantic activity of a trapped animal seeking an escape. He may join one of over two thousand ultraconservative organizations that will guarantee him political and financial security! If a churchman, he will adjure his minister: "Young man, preach the gospel, not politics!" Every news report of international importance seems to buttress the thought that international conspiracy and intrigue are determined to destroy his nation and *him*. In extreme cases he too can become mentally ill, and his paranoid delusions of persecution—"they are controlling, tormenting, threatening to kill me"—are familiar to every psychotherapist. His anxiety rules his life, dominates his thinking and destroys any capacity he has for living joyously in the present. Here again Fromm's contention that many people die before they really begin to live is seen to be so accurate. Guilt and anxiety can kill, but long before they bring about our death they have drawn out all the juice from life. The past crowds into the present with its guilt. The future also presses into our lives with anxiety. The result is that present time all but disappears, squeezed out of existence. One can test this thesis with the simple experiment of measuring as carefully as possible the fantasy (daydreaming) life of an average day. In brief: how much time do you spend worrying about what is irretrievably past, and anxiously wondering about the possibilities of tomorrow? Psychologists hold that fantasy, or daydreaming, is a good thing, provided it is kept within limits, used constructively as in meditation. Far too much fantasy deals with guilt for the past and anxiety for the future with its unknown terrors and danger.

It is small wonder, then, that so many people live lives barren of love. To paraphrase Fromm, one can say that so many people die (long before they are buried) because they do not learn to love. Present time is the only possible "place" where one can love, receive love, and transmit its supreme energy. Love cannot properly be defined. It really does not need definition any more than "food" needs to be defined. Without food we starve and die physically. Without love we suffer malnourishment of the self and we die spiritually. Tillich has said that love is unconditional because there is nothing that could condition it by a higher principle. In other words there is nothing greater than love which is the meaning of grace. Tillich writes: "Love accepts that which is unacceptable and love renews the old being so that it becomes a new being . . . grace is at the same time, the love which forgives and accepts." A most intriguing thing about love is that today it is the place where theology and psychology meet. These two disciplines are often at loggerheads with each other for a variety of reasons, one of which is semantic. When theological concepts such as grace and sin are redefined as love, and missing the mark (or self-centeredness), the psychologist can relax and take another look at them. He now can see their validity in a new context— the area in which he too is functioning both as a human being in need of love and as a psychotherapist enacting love, with a nonjudgmental sensitivity to the needs of his patient. Fully aware of the negative side of his dividedness that also includes his sin and the fact that he feels acceptable in spite of sin, he can enter into the suffering of the patient who is slowly being destroyed by his dividedness.

Love heals! But where is one to find time for love in a busy, rushed life? It is easy enough to say, "Let the past take care of the past with its guilt," and to command the future to remain in its not-yet stage and keep its anxiety there. The complete self nevertheless progressively manages to accomplish the feat of holding off past and future in order to live more adequately in the present with time for love. I think he does this because he has learned that his religion is not merely something to believe, but that it represents powerful forces that can heal and enrich life as love does.

Long before the Chinese doctor wrote her haunting book *Love Is a Many-Splendoured Thing,* the letter to the Corinthians portrayed the full spectrum of the many colors of love: "If I . . . have not love, I am a noisy gong or a clanging cymbal. . . . Love is patient and kind; love is not jealous or boastful; it is not arrogant or rude. Love does not insist on its own way, it is not irritable or resentful; it does not rejoice at wrong, but rejoices in the right. Love bears all things, believes all things, hopes all things, endures all things. Love never ends." These lines are considered by agnostic and believer alike to belong to the great literature of the world. They are probably, next to the Lord's Prayer and the Twenty-third Psalm, the most familiar section of the Bible. But the very familiarity blurs the message and breeds a sentimentalism foreign to the tough-mindedness of Paul. The most vulgar thing in the Bible about love was written by Paul: "It is better to marry than to burn." He surely had problems when he dipped his pen in acid to write that! Had he written no further on love I never would read another word of his and would like to have referred him to a psychiatrist. His love poem in Corinthians snaps him back into focus for me.

The masterful psychological acumen of Paul is seen also near the conclusion of the passage on love: "When I was a child, I spoke like a child, I thought like a child, I reasoned like a child; when I became a man, I gave up childish ways." This sentence is interspersed between two statements on knowledge and knowing one another. Here the apostle makes a deliberate connection between childhood weakness, fantasy, dependency, and development and the full spectrum and splendor of love. To become adult one must give up childish behavior; to be adult means to love. Childish love is necessarily in large part self-centered, though often its generous, outgoing, forgiving nature can embarrass grown-ups who so often are so stingy with love. Adult love needs the muscles of manhood to utilize its full energy. Everyone really knows that love is one thing that you can give away and still have more left.

The conclusion of Paul's lyric poem on love is most familiar: "So faith, hope, love abide, these three; but the greatest of these is love." Emil Brunner has suggested that these are "time-words," that when they are integrated into our life they enable us to have the proper perspective on past, present, and future. Faith handles the past for us, its guilt is seen as forgiven, the unacceptable in a man is still accepted by all who love: one's parents, wife, children, friends, God! If the agnostic reacts against the word "faith," confusing it with belief in certain concepts, let him use its synonym: "trust." Everyone trusts the banking system to the extent that he handles past debts by accepting a piece of paper, a check from his employer, which he deposits and then writes other pieces of paper to pay his bills. Trust works as effectively in the more emotional, dynamic area of life. Viktor Frankl has said that if a man has ever just once known love, he never can be deprived of that experience. Because love is strong enough to stand the shock of the unacceptable, and is seer enough to see the potentiality of one, it has reserve energy to accept completely. This is because love knows no conditions which must be met before one loves. The mistakes of conditional "love" were discussed in an earlier chapter. Love itself always is unconditional. When this is incorporated into the fiber of our being we then can trust. Then only does the past recede into the past, placed back where it correctly belongs. Guilt and remorse now cannot crowd the present.

The power that prevents the future from pressing in upon us with anxiety is hope. Here no synonym is defensively demanded of the theologian, for articles and books on the "psychology of hope" are now appearing in abundance. Psychotherapy looks with growing interest at the power of hope and future time to motivate us. The negative and self-destroying capacity of anxiety is controlled, minimized, and often overpowered by hope. Despite dark forces, threatened crises in the future, there also are men of integrity and God in the future. The men who have come to terms with death, which is part of the future for all, are, as Heidegger urges, those who really live. Most of the world's creative people have been able to face the future with those hopeful attitudes that controlled their anxiety and despair. When anxiety subsides, the future returns to the place where it belongs and no longer does it consume the time of the present. Guilt and anxiety riding out of past and future can mercilessly squeeze a life just as two horsemen of the sheriff's posse can catch a hapless demonstrator between them. When trust becomes a way of relating to people as well as to the past, and hope becomes an integral part of our world view, we will find that our present has been extended considerably. We then will have time to live, time to love, time to experience the pains and pleasures of the full spectrum of love. Love, and love alone, puts us on the way to the complete self with its victory over phoniness. Self-love, sexual love, parental love, and love in the contours of respect, concern, and commitment for community will be immeasurably enhanced, as we begin to live. The complete self is not to be viewed as a static achievement to be attained at a given point in time. It is more of a dynamic goal, a beckoning, a road sign assuring one that he is traveling in the right direction through and beyond time.

9

SUMMARY

PHONINESS, as the term is used in the preceding chapters, rarely is a result of deliberate role-playing. Rather, it is the facade raised to conceal the lack of a complete personality. The "escape from phoniness," therefore, may be achieved only by completing one's personal development so that the facade no longer is needed.

While our culture has placed a premium on some varieties of phoniness, we are reaping an inevitable reaction as naïve youth perceives and rejects the false notes in our society. Yet youth in turn will grow into its own falseness unless we can isolate and learn to cope with the personal deficiencies that make it necessary to wear a mask to hide the hollowness that lies behind it. If those deficiencies are as fundamental as I have suggested, then the curative process demands that most painful of experiences: self-revelation.

An overwhelming body of scientific evidence now supports the intuitive belief that affection—love—is the key element in the development of a complete personality. It follows that the child who grows up in a home devoid of genuine affection is very likely to become an insecure, despairing adult, himself incapable of giving real love because his own self-image is so weak and distorted. Significantly in people who have been so deprived of love and security in childhood we find the ultimate in phoniness, delinquency, violence, and reliance on what are now so popularly called "phallic symbols." These are ways of acting out unreal roles and of disguising the essential fear felt as a result of the ever-present (but never admitted) lack of security in a real role, a secure status in the community of man. Can these literally lost souls achieve that integrity of personality which is associated with maturity?

An affirmative answer requires recognition of the fact that each individual has a genuine potential for change, and that the realization of this potential is in actuality a matter of personal choice. This freedom of choice, which is the essence of humanity, is represented by man's mastery of his environment. More and more, modern man rejects alike both religious determinism and the scientific determinism implicit in a primitive Freudian view of the constricting role of early life. Man is not, as I have shown, a mere subject for the manipulation either of accidental or deliberate outside forces. Where he has the will he has the capacity to choose his own destiny.

It is impossible to overemphasize the importance of "will" or, as Frankl might put it, "attitude." There is no one who does not stand in some danger of being trapped by his anxieties, by the frustrations created by an increasingly impersonal society. Too often we see this anxiety result in a vicious circle in which anxiety produces the self-fulfilling prophecy of failure, which in turn produces hostility, guilt feelings, and then still greater anxiety and tension. Given the will—and the courage—the cycle can be broken by an honest self-assessment of the causes of the anxiety. The courage required may be great, since self-assessment and self-revelation must often be made to another person in a formal or informal therapy situation. It is precisely the necessary trust that may be lacking as a result of a childhood devoid of the trust and security derived from love. However, the courage and honesty to face and to reveal can be found in the realization that man is, indeed, "but little lower than God"; that unlike any other creature, he has the capacity to step back from his immediate circumstances, appraise both himself and his situation, and—by the mere appraisal—change his life. A person discovers that anxieties dissipate in the harsh light of honesty, as he sees that good and bad, "higher" and "lower," conflict and tension, are part of the normal human experience. Our conflicts and failures are not unique, but are, rather, a necessary reflection of our humanity. Faced and understood, these sources of anxiety are no longer disabling. Armed with understanding of the very humanity of our weaknesses, we need not expend energy on guilt, but are freed to realize our creative potentials.

Acceptance of the ubiquity of conflict—internal as well as external—also results in an ability to cope with each conflict-situation honestly, growing in the experience, instead of subconsciously avoiding the difficulty by regression, blocking, or circumnavigating the unpleasant reality. Too often in American family life we raise children to believe that conflict is per se wrong. But viewed existentially as an inherent part of human imperfection, each conflict can become an opportunity. Avoiding neither the tension nor the opportunity, the growing person adds to his store of experience and abilities to cope.

What all this adds up to, therefore, is a new sort of personal responsibility: a responsibility to self, in the fulfillment of which we also meet our responsibilities to others. Whether viewed (as by Sartre) as the ultimate responsibility, in default of a living God to share it, or (as by Frankl) as a divinely imposed duty to find and realize a personal meaning in life, we recognize an obligation to life itself, as long as it lasts. We know that this responsibility can be met, by attitude alone, when all else is beyond our control. We know also that in the acceptance of this responsibility, which is part of our humanity, we can transcend immediate circumstance and discover both meaning in life and the means to live it fully.

Perhaps this, then, is what I mean by the "complete self": the person who has faced the responsibilities that the freedom of choice imposes upon him, and thus has freed himself to *live*. He has learned that life can be lived only in the present if it is to be really lived at all. He is then neither preoccupied with the guilt for yesterday's failures, nor paralyzed by foreboding fear over tomorrow's uncertainties. His self-assurance and his awareness that he is a complete person rather than a hollow suit of armor or a ceremonial mask make it possible for him to give—and to receive—love.

Here again we can perceive a self-sustaining cycle, but this time one to be broken into instead of out of! For love-received is the source of self-assurance from which flows the courage to face hard truths and wrestle with them. In turn, an integration of personality results that makes it possible for us to expose our vulnerabilities, as we must, in order to give love; and love given is the wellspring of love received. Thus love—given and received—is an essential element in our quest for a complete self. Perhaps it does not matter at which point this cycle is broken into, but the giving and accepting of love may well be the most momentous acts that will put us on the way to self-fulfillment.